Albert Brooks: Interviews

Conversations with Filmmakers Series
Gerald Peary, General Editor

ALBERT
BROOKS

I N T E R V I E W S

Edited by Alexander Greenhough

University Press of Mississippi / Jackson

Publication of this work was made possible in part due to a subvention from
Stanford University.

The University Press of Mississippi is the scholarly publishing agency of
the Mississippi Institutions of Higher Learning: Alcorn State University,
Delta State University, Jackson State University, Mississippi State University,
Mississippi University for Women, Mississippi Valley State University,
University of Mississippi, and University of Southern Mississippi.

www.upress.state.ms.us

The University Press of Mississippi is a member
of the Association of University Presses.

Library of Congress Cataloging-in-Publication Data

Names: Greenhough, Alexander, editor.
Title: Albert Brooks : interviews / edited by Alexander Greenhough.
Other titles: Conversations with filmmakers series.
Description: Jackson : University Press of Mississippi, 2024. | Series: Conversations with
    filmmakers series | Includes filmography.
Identifiers: LCCN 2023038213 (print) | LCCN 2023038214 (ebook) | ISBN 9781496849977 (hardback) |
    ISBN 9781496849984 (trade paperback) | ISBN 9781496849991 (epub) |
    ISBN 9781496850003 (epub) | ISBN 9781496850010 (pdf) | ISBN 9781496850027 (pdf)
Subjects: LCSH: Brooks, Albert, 1947—Interviews. | Motion picture producers and
    directors—United States—Interviews. | Comedians—United States—Interviews. |
    Motion pictures—Production and direction—United States.
Classification: LCC PN1998.3.B7595 G74 20245 (print) | LCC PN1998.3.B7595 (ebook) |
    DDC 791.4302/33092 [B]—dc23/eng/20231204
LC record available at https://lccn.loc.gov/2023038213
LC ebook record available at https://lccn.loc.gov/2023038214

British Library Cataloging-in-Publication Data available

Contents

Introduction

"I don't do normal human emotions." That's Albert Brooks on his 1975 conceptual comedy album, *A Star Is Bought*. Or, that is, "Albert Brooks," his alter ego who made up such absurd, funny nonsense throughout the seventies. In sly self-reference, Brooks promoted this LP while "sick in bed" in one of the six shorts he made for the first season of *Saturday Night Live*. Exhausted from supposed overexertion, "Albert Brooks" addresses the viewer while zooming the lens in and out on himself with a remote control. He speaks with his doctor over the phone, has food delivered, then wraps things up by complaining about the quality of the film print itself, accusing a lab technician of crummy work. The shot's awkward ugliness mirrors his abrasive self-absorption, representative of Brooks's bold critique of show business.

Brooks committed himself to this obnoxious character during the first part of his career—from his six-page piece "Albert Brooks' Famous School for Comedians" for *Esquire* in 1971 to his feature debut, *Real Life* in 1979, a satire of cinéma vérité in which "Albert Brooks" makes a disastrous documentary about an ordinary middle-class family. After *Real Life*, Brooks dropped the persona ("Albert Brooks" would reappear much later in *Looking for Comedy in the Muslim World*), but he remained confrontational. In *Modern Romance*, his character's obsessive behavior baffled both studio bosses and test audiences, prompting Patrick Goldstein to title his 1981 *Los Angeles Times* piece "Mr. Nice Guy, He Is Not." Brooks told the reporter that audiences either loved or hated him and that one should "take risks and not be afraid to disturb people."

This attitude has shaped Brooks's career as an actor-writer-director. His subsequent films—*Lost in America, Defending Your Life, Mother, The Muse,* and *Looking for Comedy in the Muslim World*—are made up of the stuff which Hollywood usually hides: anxiety, conceitedness, foolishness, and failure. Brooks's insecure, confused, and sometimes angry protagonists usually end up in ironically farcical situations. Although *Defending Your Life* and *Mother* conclude happily, Brooks has always been out of step with a business which demands accessibility. That's an unusual achievement in Hollywood, given the pressure to make profitable movies. Brooks revealed to Paul Slansky in 1983 that "I enjoy making three people laugh as much as I enjoy making [three million] people laugh. It's just that, businesswise, three is not quite as impressive a number to a large studio. . . . To me, the satisfaction is not in numbers. It's that I'm making sense to other living human beings." Brooks's humor may be exasperatingly excruciating for many, but if you're one of those three people, who're into his kind of dark ridiculousness, he might indeed be, as Slansky proposed, "the funniest white man in America."

In every interview or profile in this book there's something that'll make you laugh. How about Brooks's idea for Arnold Schwarzenegger doing *Young F.D.R?* "Eleanors! I need you upstairs here! De Pearl Harbors is getting crazy vit de t'ings. Eleanors!" This observation about Saddam Hussein? "I can't imagine that anybody who chops people's hands off has a good sex life." Or, his deadpan answer to Terry Gross's earnest question about the significance of his ethnicity while shooting *Looking for Comedy in the Muslim World* in India? "I have my 'I'm Jewish' florescent hat. But I left that in Los Angeles." Maybe you'd laugh even harder if you heard that last one, rather than read it, as the wry inflection is somewhat lost in the transcription. But these pieces provide a feel for Brooks's verbal dynamism—a remarkable range of accents, tones, and voices, often presented in the form of asides and snippets of remembered and imagined conversations.

Much of his humor is discursive. Brooks has adroitly played with direct address, for instance, throughout his career. The *Albert Brooks' Famous School for Comedians* film, his *Saturday Night Live* shorts, the *Real Life* and *The Muse* trailers, and his 2016 video for a Netflix program of his films are all prime examples that open with the not quite straight-faced greeting, "Hello, I'm Albert Brooks." Paul Slansky and Bill Zehme both highlight a renowned 1973 appearance on *The Tonight Show*, where "Albert Brooks" confesses he's run out of material. "Here I am," he begins, "five years into my career, I have no more material left." He explains that although he doesn't want to be there on the show, he's received pressure from "agents, managers, pimps" who have reminded him that "if you don't go on TV they're going to forget your face." He then pulls down his pants, rips off his shirt to reveal a drawing on his chest, then covers himself with eggs, a pound cake, seltzer, and whipped cream. He emphatically insists that "this isn't the real me," as his actual work as a comedian has "quality behind it," and that this clownishness does not represent the "real" him.

Who, then, is the real Albert Brooks? He is brainy. He is funny. He can be intense. He is fascinated by humor. And, apparently, cows. Brooks likes making phone calls, and talks on the phone a lot. Much has been made of the different places he's lived over the years, in Los Angeles, because it seems like he's often at home, watching TV. Or driving his car. Since 2011, when he first logged in to promote his novel *2030*, he's shared his thoughts via Twitter. It's no secret he's liberal. But Brooks is guarded and protects his privacy. Before his marriage to artist Kimberly Shlain in the late nineties, with whom he has two children, he was circumspect about his romantic relationships, and he's never sought the limelight for its own sake.

The connection between the actual Brooks and his feature film characters is a topic of conversation in many encounters with critics and journalists. In Goldstein's article, *Real Life* producer Penelope Spheeris says, "He's exactly the same person who ends up on the screen." Brooks has pushed back against such a literal correspondence. "People always like to think everything's you," he explained to Gavin Smith in 1999, and that, in reference to *Lost in America*, he tells people: "'I don't own a motorhome, I've never lost all my money in Las Vegas, I've never worked for an ad agency, but sure, why not?' I'm not interesting enough on my own that you'd want to see a film about me." Yet it's clear that much of Brooks's work reflects what he's experienced. "Well, there must be some correlation" with his life, he pointed out to Joe Rhodes the same year, "or why would I be doing it?"

The key points in Brooks's life recur across the interviews and profiles collected here. He was born in 1947 and named Albert Einstein (a joke!) by his show-business parents Harry Einstein, a dialect comedian who performed as Parkyakarkus, and former actress Thelma Leeds, who'd appeared on screen in the mid-1930s. The pair met on the set of *New Faces of 1937* in New York. Einstein worked with Eddie Cantor on radio, and later had his own show, *Meet Me at Parky's*, in the 1940s, and appeared on television and in films. By the time Brooks was being raised with brothers Bob (also a comedian and actor, best known as Super Dave Osborne) and Cliff (an advertising executive who has appeared in many of Brooks's films) in Beverly Hills, Einstein was retired and in poor health. Harry Einstein's death on stage at the Friars Club in 1958, after a roast of Lucille Ball and Desi Arnaz, became legendary in Hollywood. Obviously, it was a pivotal event for Albert Brooks. "The interesting thing," he stressed to Bill Zehme in 1991, was that his father "*finished*. That's what makes you believe in something. Whatever reason death comes, something is here to make us finish. He didn't die in the middle of a line, and that's something." Its meaning affected Brooks's reflections on the afterlife, too, influencing the conception of *Defending Your Life*. To interviewer Robert DiMatteo, he noted that "my father died when I was eleven years old, so . . . I got some extra years thinking, gee, where did Dad go? And I never liked the concept of heaven and hell—it was so black and white."

Brooks later attended Beverly Hills High School and was seen as preternaturally hilarious. Comic legend Carl Reiner, the father of classmate and friend Rob Reiner, considered him a prodigy; when Johnny Carson asked Reiner on *The Tonight Show* who the funniest person he knew was, Reiner replied, "a sixteen-year-old kid named Albert Einstein." He initially wanted to act, studying at Carnegie Mellon for a couple of years, but began work as a comedian due to a lack of available roles. Unusually, he started out on television, not in clubs, specializing in portraying talentless, incompetent performers, perhaps most notably Danny and Dave, the world's worst ventriloquist, on shows such as *The Steve Allen Show*, *The Dean Martin Show*, and *The Ed Sullivan Show*.

In 1971, Brooks began playing a version of himself with his fake advertisement for "Albert Brooks' Famous School for Comedians" in *Esquire*, which he adapted into a short film of the same title for the PBS series *The Great American Dream Machine*, soon after appearing on *The Tonight Show* in the first of many appearances throughout the decade, including that great bit about the "real me" in 1973. Brooks toured the country during this period, often opening for Neil Diamond and Sly and the Family Stone, before a notorious "meltdown" at a Boston comedy club the same year, at which point he stopped performing live. He released two comedy albums—*Comedy Minus One* and *A Star Is Bought*—and made six short films for the debut season of *Saturday Night Live* in 1975 and 1976, which he wrote, directed, and appeared in as "Albert Brooks." Since the *SNL* shorts, he has starred in and written all of the films he's directed, from *Real Life* to *Looking for Comedy in the Muslim World*.

Brooks works in the tradition of the comedy actor-writer-director that began with Mack Sennett, Charlie Chaplin, Buster Keaton, and continued with auteurs such as Jerry Lewis, Mel Brooks, and Woody Allen. Brooks has frequently been likened to Allen, the comparison beginning early. It's in Goldstein's 1981 *Los Angeles Times* profile, which was published a month after a brief piece by Bruce McCabe in the *Boston Globe* entitled "Albert Brooks: A West Coast Woody Allen." There are obvious similarities; both men are cerebral, Jewish, and began as comedians, whose films reflexively explore the worries and doubts of creative types.

Yet there are many differences. An obvious contrast is their respective personal lives. Allen's is extraordinarily controversial, while Brooks's is not. Unlike Allen, Brooks isn't prolific, with an oeuvre which is distinctly and decidedly consistent: he stars in all his films, which he's cowritten with only one collaborator, Monica Johnson, with the exception of *Defending Your Life* and *Looking for Comedy in the Muslim World*, which he penned solo. Though just twelve years younger, Brooks belongs to an entirely different generation—he's a Baby Boomer, whose mock-epic *Lost in America* dramatized the impossibility of living according to the hippie ethos within Reagan's "trickle-down" America. While Brooks has alluded to his Jewishness throughout his career, it's arguably an undercurrent until *Looking for Comedy in the Muslim World*, with its sharp exchange where a woman suspiciously eyes "Albert Brooks" up and asks, "You're not a Jew, are you?" to which he replies, "Not this minute." With Allen, such a question would be redundant, what with all those rabbi jokes. And Brooks's cultural references are not highbrow; as he pointed out to Goldstein, if *Modern Romance* were an Allen movie, the toy giraffe Robert picks up for Mary would be a novel. In that piece, Brooks may quip that he's trying to be taken less seriously than Allen, but this is disingenuous.

Brooks takes himself seriously. He's very selective, for instance, about roles he'll play in other directors' films. Though he's had memorable turns in films such as *Taxi Driver*, *Twilight Zone: The Movie*, *Broadcast News*, *The Scout* (which he cowrote with Johnson), *My First Mister*, and *Drive*, not to mention voicing Marlin in Pixar's *Finding Nemo* and *Finding Dory*, Brooks has passed on so many—including leads in major box-office hits such as *When Harry Met Sally* and *Pretty Woman*—that *Vulture* published "The Lost Roles of Albert Brooks" in 2011. Aside from some vocal performances for *The Simpsons*, a four-episode run on *Weeds* in 2008, playing "Albert Brooks" in one episode of *Curb Your Enthusiasm* in 2021, and a few talk-show and award-show appearances, Brooks has been completely absent from television since the 1970s. Bill Zehme suggested in the early 1990s that some in Hollywood conjectured that Brooks might have a fear of success. There may be something to that, as he has purposefully critiqued celebrity culture right from the start, but his selectivity is as much about artistic integrity. His "minimum crap record," as he described it to David Handelman, is the result of being, at times, uncompromising with executives and studios. He had a bumpy relationship with producer Lorne Michaels at *Saturday Night Live*, wouldn't make specific cuts to *Modern Romance*, prompting Columbia Pictures to limit its release to a few big cities, and was dropped by the initial distributor of *Looking for Comedy in the Muslim World*, Sony Pictures, when he refused to remove "Muslim" from the title. As he put it to Joe Rhodes in 1999: "The business and I never embraced each other."

Brooks consistently bemoans the Hollywood obsession with box office. He's annoyed that film comedy isn't taken seriously as an art form and that there's been a dumbing down of this genre, which has become overly formulaic. He's often compared this standardization to the appeal of McDonald's, but with David Elliot, who reported on *Lost in America* in 1985, he used another food analogy. "It's like, say you eat Velveeta and like it," Brooks said. "And I give you some fine Swiss cheese that's a little tart. The first time you'll probably say, 'Yecch,' but maybe by the third or fourth time you'll like it, and your brain will figure out, 'Gee, the tartness is what makes it better.' It's the same with art, but if kids aren't given any better, how can they reject *Porky's Revenge*? So the studios turn around and say—this is my least favorite argument—'They're buying, so give them what they like.'"

For an elaboration on this point, where Brooks argues that film reviewing is like a "consumer report, like when you buy a Ford," check out the 1993 *BUZZ* piece. It's all in his own words. Uncommonly, in the land of the blockbuster, you'll find an American filmmaker state that popular and good are not "necessarily synonymous." He praises Stanley Kubrick's *2001: A Space Odyssey* as much for its daring ambiguity as its visionary images, noting that Hollywood filmmakers "are so afraid that if the audience doesn't understand a hundred percent of a movie all the time, you've done something wrong." The reference to this specific film probably isn't accidental. Kubrick admired *Modern Romance*, and the two filmmakers kept up a telephonic friendship for years, detailed in David Handelman's 1997 profile. While Handelman makes the familiar Woody Allen comparison, Brooks himself draws a parallel with Kubrick in their limited output. They both make ironic, concept-driven films, too. Yet Kubrick mounts lavishly budgeted genre films with A-list stars, adapted (with many coscenarists) from short stories and novels. Resemblance will thus only get you so far in making sense of an auteur like Brooks, whether it's Allen or Kubrick or anyone else.

   Albert Brooks's work is based on Albert Brooks. Or, at least, what he's been reflecting upon, and what he thinks is funny. He is his own genre. Extrapolating from his experiences, Brooks reflexively entwines performance and persona. Showbiz self-consciousness is nothing new; it goes as far back as Buster Keaton's *Sherlock Jr.*, and Brooks has often cited the self-referential, low-key Jack Benny as a major influence. Yet Brooks's innovative twist on this tendency turns on his own career in Tinseltown. His protagonists all work in dream factories of one kind or another: a comedian and filmmaker (*Real Life, Looking for Comedy in the Muslim World*), a film editor (*Modern Romance*), a screenwriter (*The Muse*), an adman (*Lost in America, Defending Your Life*), and a science fiction novelist (*Mother*). He's not, however, simply making "movies about movies." With sophisticated anti-illusionistic distanciation and intertextual references, Brooks wittily scrutinizes the mass media, exposing a system determined by social and economic forces to which he's subjected, too, as a performer. "I don't try to remake the world. I just try to live in it," he told Joe Rhodes.

   As a writer and director, Brooks has a commensurate ear and eye for authenticity. This move to naturalism seems oddly fitting for an artist who spent a decade faking things on network television, whose "Albert Brooks" burnt the Yeager home down in a demented homage to *Gone with the Wind* at the end of *Real Life*. You can trace his desire for verisimilitude throughout this book. He's concerned with plausibility: "I don't see many explosions or ten-car crashes in the course of my life," Brooks stated to Paul Slansky in 1983, "so I don't put them into my movies." He wants performances to be convincing; when casting *Mother*, according to David Handelman's reporting, Brooks went with Debbie Reynolds instead of Esther Williams because he didn't want the latter "to have to act a person that she wasn't." The visual style he's developed is accordingly observational. As he explained to Gavin Smith, "I've always sort of imagined movies as people looking through a window. Sort of peeping in on the goings-on." When

I asked him to expand on this in 2018, Brooks made the relation between form and content clear. "Everything needs to disappear in service of the story," he said, adding, "I want a sense of reality. I want a sense of believability."

Brooks's oeuvre is packed with all-too-familiar misunderstandings, frustrations, and disappointments, but also moments of hopefulness, delight, and pleasure. Feelings propel Brooks's narratives. Consider, for example, jealousy in *Modern Romance*, anger in *Lost in America*, sadness in *Mother*, and, of course, fear in *Defending Your Life*. They're not as one-dimensional or neatly delineated as this short list suggests, for his characters' emotions are compounded and complex. Despite, or perhaps because of, its otherworldly setting, *Defending Your Life* feels truthful in this regard, and is very much an emotional portrait. While fear is its main operative emotion, Daniel (Albert Brooks) experiences the joy of romantic love with the luminous Julia (Meryl Streep)—the excitement of mutual attraction, the intensity of desire, and the contentment of attachment. The film exalts in a simple phrase: "I love you." But other shades are mixed in there. Daniel is envious of Julia's confidence and bravery, her fancy accommodations, and the ease of her "trial" in Judgment City. There's smugness, anxiety, and shame as well—and, when Daniel tries the revolting meal of Bob Diamond (Rip Torn), a brilliant display of disgust.

These feelings are common, regardless of what sparks them. "I've always hated the word *neurotic*—life is not an easy road for anybody no matter who you are," Brooks noted in Gavin Smith's interview. Through his self-referential and self-conscious approach, he explores the ubiquitous aspects of everyday life—family, relationships, leisure, work—from the underlining assumption that there's an intense need for human connection through humor. It's a need Brooks himself clearly has, even if his audience is just one person on the other end of the line. (For poets and novelists, there are the collected letters; with Brooks, one wishes for the collected phone calls.) In the same interview, Brooks described film directing as having "all the choices." By remaining true to his vision and maintaining his autonomy—in Hollywood, of all places!—Albert Brooks has managed to present, across his work as a writer, performer, and director, not just those "normal human emotions" he joked about early on, but all the emotions.

This book began in 2017 as an amiable conversation with the director of the University Press of Mississippi, Craig Gill, at the Society for Cinema and Media Studies conference in Chicago. I'm grateful to him for commissioning the volume. Throughout the process of ascertaining the rightsholders of the interviews, securing permissions, and assembling the manuscript, the Press's Emily Bandy has consistently provided timely guidance and advice. I'm appreciative of her patience and support.

At Stanford University, in the Program in Writing and Rhetoric (PWR) and ITALIC, I'm fortunate to work with kind and entertaining colleagues who've shown interest in this project—thank you, Karla Oeler, Kim Beil, Ryan Tacata, Nicholas Jenkins, Sam Sax, and Lisa Swan for all the great conversations. Marvin Diogenes, the program director of PWR, read a draft of the introduction and continues to generously share his insights into American comedy with me. PWR's administrative coordinator Cristina Huerta provided indispensable assistance managing research funds used for this project.

My thanks to Jessica Thompson, Albert Brooks's assistant, who set up the phone interview, and to Albert Brooks for taking the time to discuss his film-making and for checking the book's chronology for accuracy.

Fellow *Modern Romance* enthusiast Elric Kane has periodically checked in on my progress, as has my mother, Marlo Greenhough, a *Broadcast News* fan; I've benefited from their encouragement. And a big, big thank you to my wife, Jenny Greenhough, for all her care and love, and my son, Samuel, who at age ten really enjoys the "3D" *Real Life* trailer. Their jokes and laughter are a constant delight.

AG

Chronology

1947   Born Albert Einstein on July 22 to Thelma Leeds and Harry Einstein in Beverly Hills, California.

1960–65 Attends Beverly Hills High School. Classmates include Richard Dreyfuss, Rob Reiner, and Larry Bishop (son of comedian Joey Bishop), with whom Brooks works in a comedy duo.

1966–68 Attends Carnegie Mellon University, where he studies acting.

1968   First television appearance, on *Keene at Noon*, a Los Angeles talk show, performing Danny and Dave. Appearances on *The Steve Allen Show*.

1969–70 Appearances on *The Dean Martin Show*, *The Merv Griffin Show*, *The Everly Brothers Show*, *Dean Martin Presents the Golddiggers*, and several other variety shows.

1971   Appearances on several variety shows, including *The Flip Wilson Show*, *The Ed Sullivan Show*, *The Johnny Cash Show*, and the first of many on *The Tonight Show Starring Johnny Carson*. "Albert Brooks' Famous School for Comedians" published in *Esquire*. Begins performing stand-up live at comedy clubs and as the opening act for rock and pop musicians.

1972   *Albert Brooks' Famous School for Comedians*, a short film adaptation of the *Esquire* piece, is broadcast on the variety television series *The Great American Dream Machine*.

1973   Release of comedy album, *Comedy Minus One*. Stops performing live.

1975   Release of comedy album, *A Star Is Bought*.

1975–76 Makes six short films—*Home Movies*, *The Impossible Truth*, *NBC Super Season*, *Heart Surgery*, *Sick in Bed*, and *The National Audience Research Institute*—that are broadcast on the first season of *Saturday Night Live*.

1976   Appears in Martin Scorsese's *Taxi Driver*, his first feature film performance.

1979   Release of his debut feature film, *Real Life*.

2016   Voices Marlin in Andrew Stanton's *Finding Dory*. Voices Tiberius in Chris Renaud and Yarrow Cheney's *The Secret Life of Pets*. Netflix streams all of Brooks's feature films. Release, on YouTube, of short promotional film, *A Message to Netflix from Albert Brooks*.

2021   Appears in the television series *Curb Your Enthusiasm*.

2023   Appears in Rob Reiner's *Albert Brooks: Defending My Life*.

Filmography

REAL LIFE (1979)
Paramount Pictures
Director: **Albert Brooks**
Screenplay: **Albert Brooks**, Monica Johnson, Harry Shearer
Producer: Penelope Spheeris
Cinematography: Eric Saarinen
Editor: David Finfer
Music: Mort Lindsey
Cast: **Albert Brooks**, Charles Grodin, Frances Lee McCain, J. A. Preston,
Matthew Tobin, Jennings Lang
98 minutes

MODERN ROMANCE (1981)
Columbia Pictures
Director: **Albert Brooks**
Screenplay: **Albert Brooks**, Monica Johnson
Producer: Andrew Scheinman, Martin Shafer
Cinematography: Eric Saarinen
Editor: David Finfer
Music: Lance Rubin
Cast: **Albert Brooks**, Kathryn Harrold, Bruno Kirby, James L. Brooks,
Bob Einstein, Meadowlark Lemon, George Kennedy
93 minutes

LOST IN AMERICA (1985)
The Geffen Company/Warner Bros.
Director: **Albert Brooks**
Screenplay: **Albert Brooks**, Monica Johnson
Producer: Marty Katz
Cinematography: Eric Saarinen
Editor: David Finfer
Music: Arthur B. Rubinstein

Cast: **Albert Brooks**, Julie Hagerty, Garry Marshall, Michael Greene, Tom Tarpey, Art Frankel, Joey Coleman
91 minutes

DEFENDING YOUR LIFE (1991)
Geffen Pictures/Warner Bros.
Director: **Albert Brooks**
Screenplay: **Albert Brooks**
Producer: Michael Grillo
Cinematography: Allen Daviau
Editor: David Finfer
Music: Michael Gore
Cast: **Albert Brooks**, Meryl Streep, Rip Torn, Lee Grant, Buck Henry
111 minutes

MOTHER (1996)
Paramount Pictures
Director: **Albert Brooks**
Screenplay: **Albert Brooks**, Monica Johnson
Producer: Scott Rudin, Herb Nanas
Cinematography: Lojas Koltai
Editor: Harvey Rosenstock
Music: Marc Shaiman
Cast: **Albert Brooks**, Debbie Reynolds, Rob Morrow, John C. McGinley, Lisa Kudrow
103 minutes

THE MUSE (1999)
October Films
Director: **Albert Brooks**
Screenplay: **Albert Brooks**, Monica Johnson
Producer: Herb Nanas
Cinematography: Thomas Ackerman
Editor: Peter Teschner
Music: Elton John
Cast: **Albert Brooks**, Sharon Stone, Andie MacDowell, Jeff Bridges
97 minutes

LOOKING FOR COMEDY IN THE MUSLIM WORLD (2005)
Shangri-La Entertainment/Warner Independent Pictures
Director: **Albert Brooks**
Screenplay: **Albert Brooks**
Producer: Herb Nanas
Cinematography: Thomas Ackerman
Editor: Anita Brandt Burgoyne
Music: Michael Giacchino
Cast: **Albert Brooks**, Sheetal Sheth, John Carroll Lynch, Jon Tenney, Amy Ryan
98 minutes

Albert Brooks: Interviews

Every Kid Should Have an Albert

Paul Slansky / 1979

From the *Village Voice*, March 5, 1979, 48–49. Reprinted with permission.

On February 4, 1974, Albert Brooks walked onto the stage of *The Tonight Show* for the twenty-second time. His past performances had included some of the funniest bits ever seen on the show: an impressionist whose imitations of various celebrities all sounded like Ed Sullivan; a mime who came out in whiteface and proceeded to describe, with a French accent, his every action ("Now I am walking down ze stairs, now I am petting ze dog"); and an elephant trainer whose elephant was sick, forcing him to substitute a frog.

But this time Brooks's normally genial face wore a troubled expression. He explained that his appearance on the show was an unfortunate mistake, that he had only come because his manager insisted it was time to do another Carson show. "Let's just talk philosophy for a minute," he said earnestly. "A lot of us have a game plan. We don't want to give too much of ourselves too quickly because, you know, then it's all gone. Here I am, five years into my career, and my game plan is all off. I have no material left. While you folks were having turkey dinner last week, I was down to my last bit."

This was no laughing matter, as the silent audience clearly recognized. There *had* been those rumors of a recent breakdown on stage in a Boston nightclub, and didn't Johnny always call him "Crazy Albert Brooks?" God, was the guy about to crack up on national television? A few uneasy coughs broke the silence.

He then went through a scornful recitation of all the things he *could* do if he wanted to settle for cheap laughs. Sure, he could get a laugh by dropping his pants, he said, dropping them and getting an enormous (and relieved) one. Sure, he could break people up smashing eggs on his head, but who couldn't? Sure, he could draw a funny face on his chest . . .

A few minutes later, with his pants around his ankles, whipped cream and eggs dripping from his head, a cake on his face, and a face on his chest, he stared into the camera and said, "This isn't the real me." He pulled an 8 × 10 glossy out of his

3

shorts, declared, "*This* is the real me!" and stalked offstage a la Jimmy Durante. The audience responded with a solid minute of applause.

So whatever happened to Albert Brooks? Three years ago it looked like he was going to make it big. His short films were appearing on *Saturday Night Live*. He made his motion picture debut as the pushy campaign worker in *Taxi Driver*. His second album, *A Star Is Bought*, received a Grammy nomination, and *Time* called him "the smartest, most audacious comic talent since Lenny Bruce and Woody Allen." Enormous success seemed within his grasp, if only he would reach for it. Instead, he dropped out of sight.

He has spent the past three years working on *Real Life* his first feature film which Paramount is distributing. *Real Life* is the most original American comedy in recent memory. Brooks wrote the film, with comedy writers Harry Shearer and Monica Johnson. He raised the money for it—under one million dollars—from a man who didn't even read the script. He directed it, and spent six months in the editing room with it, designed the print ad, and created the TV and radio spots. In short, total control.

"When he was younger," says Harry Shearer, "he really sat down and mapped out five-year plans—he was like a Communist government. One of the ways Albert is smarter than most of the people in the business is that he's held out for total control over the things that are important to him."

Brooks calls *Real Life* "a staged documentary comedy." In it, he plays a comedian named Albert Brooks, who joins forces with a scientific research institute and a major Hollywood studio to make a film about a year in the lives of a typical American family. (Remember the Louds?) Wall cameras sensitive to body heat, and portable devices worn over the heads of the film crew, will capture every moment's bit of activity.

The Yeagers of Phoenix, Arizona, are chosen: veterinarian Warren, his wife Jeanette, and their two children. Unsurprisingly, their lives immediately begin to fall apart under the scrutiny. Their first dinner sets the mood, with Warren and Jeanette arguing about her menstrual cramps while cameramen diligently circle the table.

Things get worse. Jeanette visits her gynecologist, whom Albert recognizes as a baby broker exposed on *60 Minutes*. Warren loses a patient—a horse. Jeanette's grandmother dies, and Warren talks about the dead horse during her funeral service. Finally, an article about the family appears in a local newspaper, and they are besieged by TV cameras whenever they leave the house. Throughout the family's ordeal Brooks reassures them, even as he manipulates them to ensure the success of the project. (When Jeanette says her children are afraid to go to school, Brooks counters, "That's normal, trust me.")

The Yeagers are victims, not villains. Their irrational desire for celebrity—and Brooks's—is the result of society's celebration of it as the only goal worth attaining. *Real Life* operates on so many levels and takes on so many subjects, with such attention to detail, that it demands to be seen more than once. Brooks's cynicism is aimed at our affectations, not our aspirations, and he trusts his audience to join him in acknowledging—and enjoying—the utter silliness of it all.

"Albert is a national treasure," says Charles Grodin, who plays Warren Yeager in the film. "I'm delighted that we're alive at the same time. I'd like to see him have everything. He's so damn good, you just have to feel that way."

When I call Albert Brooks to set up a meeting for the following day, he suggests getting together immediately. Unfortunately, my tape recorder has a dead battery, and I don't want to sit down with him without it.

"Maybe I should just jot down some of the things I might say," he says. "Okay, I'll tell you what. I'll bring a tape recorder, I'll bring batteries, I'll even bring cassettes. What size shirt do you wear?" Twenty minutes later, he walks into the El Padrino Room of the Beverly Wilshire Hotel with a recorder and a cassette of Emmylou Harris's *Elite Hotel*. "It's the only tape I could find," he says. "You've got forty minutes."

We begin by discussing the genesis of some of his early routines, including the out-of-material bit. "It was time to do another Carson show," he says, "and I really didn't have anything to do. So I thought, this is interesting, maybe I can get something out of this. Most of my bits come from what's really there. You turn it into entertainment by making it a little more interesting."

He points to a horse behind our table. "Sometimes I like to make up names for the horses of famous people," he says. "Like if Burt Bacharach had a horse, what would he call it? Maybe, 'Where's Angie?' If we stop now you get the rest of Emmylou's album, you know."

The waiter brings my drink, and a chef's salad and iced coffee for Albert, who says that he might be going to Hawaii for a vacation in a few days. "Maybe I shouldn't see you again before you go," I say. "Then I'll have to go to Hawaii to finish the piece."

"Will your editors pay for it?" he asks. "Because if they will, here's what we'll do. When you get to Hawaii, there'll be a message waiting for you saying I've gone on to Japan. Then we'll go to China, and . . ." He stops himself. "What am I talking about?" he practically moans. "I'll never leave. I've been talking about a vacation for five years, I just never leave. It's sick, it's not healthy." He suddenly brightens. "You know what I've always wanted to do? I've always wanted to put a lung in a suitcase and send it through an airport security check. In effect, the guard would be looking at an X-ray of a lung."

Aside from Albert's comic instinct, the most striking thing about him is his confidence in it. His jokes are delivered as casually as they occur to him. It's clear that if he *thinks* something is funny, he goes with it—getting a laugh is a pleasant but nonessential bonus.

"*I'll* leave the tip," Albert says loudly when the check arrives. "Not really. That was just for the tape recorder."

Two days later, I arrive at Albert's Hollywood office intending to observe an average day in his real life, but he has other plans: a trip to Magic Mountain to ride Colossus, this year's World's Largest Roller Coaster.

Albert calls Magic Mountain, lowering his voice in an approximation of the sort of simpleton who doesn't find the very notion of such hype ludicrous: "Hullo, uh, I'm not going to be coming up there, but if I were, what time does Colossus open? And how long is the wait? Thank you." He hangs up and laughs. "She said, 'It opens at three and there's a two-hour wait. Let everybody go on and then it'll clear out and you'll go later on in the evening.' She's planning our evening! 'You'll have dinner here, you'll buy bumper stickers, we got a hotel room for you . . .' Let's go."

An hour later, we pay seventeen dollars at the admission gate, stop to buy Sno-Cones, and join the line about a quarter mile from the ride. "It's amazing how this place generates absolutely no excitement of its own," Albert says. "The frightening thing would be if they said we could never leave here. Aside from all the things you'd never be able to do again, you'd have to eat every meal here."

Two young girls walk by wearing Fonzie T-shirts. "I bet half the kids in this park know the name Freddie Silverman," Albert says. "What other era could you live in where kids know the name of a head of programming?

"But I can't think of any time I'd rather be living in, because of the technology. It's just amazing." (Few of his friends understand his fascination with technology, which is much in evidence in *Real Life*. But Harry Shearer, who shares the obsession, has an explanation: "Albert is basically an optimist, and if you want to be optimistic about the future, technology is the only refuge you've got.")

"Catalina was the last place in the country to get a phone system that didn't need operators," Albert continues. "Everyone in town used to know each other through the operator, and now that way of life is gone, just gone," he says wistfully, then interrupts himself. "Who cares? I wanna go on Colossus!" He breaks into a Bob Hope parody: "Now I don't wanna say that it was a long wait, but the kid in front of me learned to read on the line. I don't wanna say I was scared, but . . . you finish it."

An hour after getting on line, we pass under the Colossus sign, and Albert begins his countdown "Six minutes, six minutes! Four minutes!" Albert screams and waves his hands in the air as our car plunges along the tracks, but the ride is unworthy of its hype. "Weightless eleven times, they said—I only counted four," he says as we walk down the ramp. "Three good drops, no good banks. If we'd waited two hours, I would have been disappointed."

We stop at a souvenir stand to buy buttons that proclaim "I RODE IT!" "Well, we rode it," Albert says, "but only because you wanted to know what my average day was like. I do it every day. See what my button says, 'I RODE IT A MILLION TIMES!'"

Looking for a place to get a salad, we pass a gift shop with a rack of dresses near the doorway. "Who buys clothes here?" Albert wonders. "'Hey, that's nice, where'd you get it?' 'Magic Mountain.'"

The salad hunt proves futile. "I didn't really want one anyway," Albert says as we leave the park. "I wanted to get the button that came with it—'I ATE SALAD AT MAGIC MOUNTAIN.'"

"Every kid should have an Albert," says comedy writer Monica Johnson. "He's the kind of person you'd want to be locked in jail with. You know, you don't have a game, you don't have any cigarettes, what could be better than having Albert Brooks in there?"

Harry Einstein (better known as Parkyakarkus, a Greek-dialect radio comedian) finally couldn't resist the joke—he named his fourth son Albert. "My father was very sick around the time I was born," says Albert, sitting in the living room of his rented Benedict Canyon home and leafing through a bound volume of Parkyakarkus's radio scripts. "The doctors thought he wouldn't live.

"He did recover, but I don't remember him as very active. I do remember lots of schtick around the dinner table. Generally, he and my brothers and I were all laughing at the same thing my mother did not find funny, whatever that was.

"I guess I was the class clown—with a name like Albert Einstein, you don't hide in the back. I'd read the school bulletin to the class and I'd add activities and make stuff up. It was good, a good ten minutes every morning."

When Harry Einstein died in 1958, eleven-year-old Albert, who had grown up around Hollywood comedians, already had a reputation among them as a budding comic genius. A few years later, when Johnny Carson asked Carl Reiner to name the funniest men he knew, Mel Brooks and a high-school kid named Albert Einstein were the two that he mentioned.

In the summer of 1965, after graduating from Beverly Hills High, Albert went to Plymouth, Massachusetts, to perform in summer stock. "Albert wanted to be a serious actor," says Rob Reiner, a close friend since high school. "He went to Carnegie Tech in Pittsburgh for its drama department and he was talking about doing all this dramatic theatre. We'd say, 'Albert, you're funny. What you do best is make people laugh." He fought that for the longest time, and finally he started doing it and liking it." He left college after three years, took the name of Brooks ("It sounded good with Albert," he says), and returned to Los Angeles to start his career.

The traditional comedy formats became his targets. The first bit he came up with was "Danny and Dave," an inept ventriloquist act that he performed on the syndicated *Steve Allen Show* in 1968. The *Dean Martin, Merv Griffin,* and *Ed Sullivan* shows followed, and other offers were coming in, but even then Albert was wary of losing control of his life.

"If I'd wanted to be a big star, I could have done the dummy bit forty times, and everyone in the country would have known me," he says. "But I didn't want to be known as the guy with the dummy, so I forced myself to keep coming up with new stuff."

In February 1971, *Esquire* ran an article called "Albert Brooks' Famous School for Comedians," a take-off on all those correspondence schools that promise to turn you into another Van Gogh if you can trace the outline of your hand. The article—which Albert later turned into a short film for PBS's *Great American Dream Machine*—presented the faculty (Joe Garagiola and Totie Fields, among others), key campus sites (the Don DeFore Mall), and the curriculum, which included courses in dialect, the double take, and the importance of choosing a disease to help eradicate. At the end came a comedy talent test which the reader could take to see if he qualified for enrollment. A sample question:

Take my wife _____.
  A. for instance. B. I'll be along later. C. please.

The magazine received over two hundred serious inquiries about the school.

He did his first *Tonight Show* in mid-1972, and quickly became a Carson favorite. Instead of adopting bizarre, negative personae that would exploit the audience's hostilities, Albert performed as himself, using his feelings rather than disguising them and talking as if the audience were sitting in his living room. So sure was he of his instincts that he didn't even audition his new material for friends. "I tried out all my stuff on national television," he says. "After doing two years of TV, I felt confident enough to put together a live act."

Albert spent three years on the road, headlining in small clubs and opening for rock stars like Neil Diamond in larger halls. The anxiety and boredom created by doing the same material night after night finally got to him during a tour to promote his first album, *Comedy Minus One*, and a gig at Paul's Mall in Boston was literally the end of the road. "I was just real tired," he says, "and the record wasn't even in the stores. I remember doing an interview with a disc jockey who said to me, 'Jonathan Winters went crazy, you think that's ever gonna happen to you?' I said, 'I think it's happening right now.'" In the middle of his one-week engagement, he flew back to LA.

Around this time, he began going out with Linda Ronstadt, a relationship that lasted two years. "I was going with Linda just before big things started happening for her," he says. "We lived together for almost a year. We liked each other because at that time we had the exact same fear of performing—whatever that fear was, we shared it."

(Albert is reluctant to discuss his personal life, but Penelope Spheeris, who produced *Real Life*, says, "Albert's women are usually real serious. His love affairs are always like *The Tempest*.")

By the end of 1975, his films were appearing regularly on *Saturday Night Live*, ostensibly the ideal vehicle to catapult him to stardom. Unfortunately, the relationship was not a smooth one.

"Albert, to put it in its mildest form, is sometimes intolerant of other people's problems," says producer Lorne Michaels. "We couldn't edit, we couldn't have audience laughter on the soundtrack. He had complete creative control. I had asked him for three-to-five-minute films, he got me up to five-to-seven minutes, and eventually they came in at ten. And you couldn't say they were too long, because he would say, 'They're brilliant.'"

Well, they *were*. *The Impossible Truth* featured an interview with a blind cab driver: "Damn right, I still drive. What should I do, sit home and collect welfare?" Another film had Albert fulfilling a lifelong dream—performing heart surgery. ("I pray it doesn't hurt, I *pray* it doesn't hurt," says the patient as Albert, who has forgotten the anesthesia, prepares to make the first incision.)

But the best of the lot was *Super Season*, an elaborately filmed parody of network promotion spots previewing scenes from three "new" shows: *Black Vet* (a Black Vietnam veteran takes up practice as a veterinarian in a small southern town); *Medical Season* ("But it's unnecessary. This man does not need surgery," a doctor says as a patient is wheeled into the operating room. Replies his colleague: "It's too late. He's already paid for it and we've already spent the money"); and *The Three of Us*, a sitcom about a man living with two women—a premise which apparently was not too ridiculous for ABC, which built a real series around it two years later.

When the six-film contract expired, neither party was inclined to renew. "Viewer mail rated my films the least popular part of the show," says Albert. "The Muppets were the audience favorites."

Instead of becoming a superstar, he went to work on *Real Life*. "The groundhog came out today, laughed, and scratched 'See *Real Life*' in the dirt," he says. "That's a good sign, isn't it?"

"You rode the ride, now hear the commercial," Albert says, as an ad for Colossus comes on the radio of his Honda Civic. A Mercedes with a "RUNNERS MAKE BETTER LOVERS" bumper sticker on its trunk moves in front of us as we drive to a Japanese restaurant for sushi, Albert's favorite food.

"Wouldn't it be great if cars came equipped with screens like that thing they have in Times Square that spells out the news?" he asks. "You could punch out your own instant messages: WILL THE SMALL RED CAR WITH THE UGLY DRIVER PLEASE STAY A LITTLE FURTHER BEHIND?"

"Night Fever" comes on the radio. "A few months ago, you literally could not turn on the radio without hearing this," he says. "If someone put a gun to your head and said, 'Find the Bee Gees in thirty seconds,' you could do it."

What about his plans for the future? "I don't know what I'm going to do next," Albert says. "I haven't started writing another film yet. I want to see what the climate is like for *Real Life* before I decide.

"It only makes me anxious when I think ahead. I mean, some things you have to plan, but if you think far enough ahead, you're dead. Hey, that sounds like a slogan. Let's put it on the bumper."

Everything is material for Albert Brooks—a lawn sprinkler watering an area of grass the size of a paper plate, a squashed coyote on the side of the road that "might just be taking a nap," the president of the United States saying that "as far as sovereignty goes, I have no hang-ups about it." His comedic vision encompasses everything he sees. Nothing is wasted, not even a pit stop to buy cassettes for the drive up to Magic Mountain, as I realize days later while transcribing my tapes.

There's Albert, talking about why he doesn't smoke or drink, describing how uncomfortable he felt the time he leased a Cadillac, saying he'll wait in the car while I get the cassettes.

And then there's this: "You're in the record store now, Paul, so this'll be a surprise for you, because right now you're buying tapes and we're going to Magic Mountain. What's going to happen is that I intend to kill you at Magic Mountain. This will happen right before we go on the ride. I'm only doing it to get new movie ideas, 'cause, you know, I owe it to the people. Bye-bye."

Brooks's "Modern" Role: Mr. Nice Guy, He Is Not

Patrick Goldstein / 1981

From the *Los Angeles Times*, May 5, 1981, G1, G4. Copyright © 1981. *Los Angeles Times*.
Used with permission.

Most comedians need to be loved. Albert Brooks will take his chances.
"As a comedian it's really my job to be the monster," said Brooks, who co-wrote, starred in, and directed *Modern Romance*. "People either love me or hate me. If I wanted to be a nice guy, I'd make a movie about someone who saves animals."

Playing the part of a neurotic Hollywood film editor in the throes of a crumbling romance, Brooks plays the bad guy—to the hilt.

An incorrigibly jealous suitor, Brooks spies on his girlfriend, traces her phone calls, wallows in a self-pitying drug haze, whines to his friends, ducks his mother's phone calls, and broods aloud about his disastrous love life.

As a Brooks fan put it: "If he wasn't so funny, he'd be an unsufferable jerk."

Brooks appeared genuinely puzzled that people view him as such an unsympathetic character. "Life isn't sympathetic," said Brooks, as droll in person as on camera. "It's a cruel world out there. Find me five sympathetic people in the world in 1981."

A comic prodigy, Brooks went to Beverly Hills High with Rob Reiner and Richard Dreyfuss. Most kids practiced their stand-up routines in front of the bathroom mirror—Brooks tried his out at Bel-Air dinner parties.

His father, Harry Einstein, was a radio dialect comedian who died when Brooks was young. "My big influence was my older brother who was 6-foot-4" (and appears in Brooks's films). Asked if they were sibling rivals, Brooks laughed. "Well, let's say he would beat me up if I rivaled him. That taught me how to be an opening act. My mother taught me how to close the show."

Before he turned twenty-one, Brooks had appeared on *The Steve Allen Show* and *The Ed Sullivan Show*. He also put in time as an opening act on the rock concert circuit. "That taught me not only the meaning of adversity, but the meaning of how to duck."

Brooks made regular appearances on *The Tonight Show* throughout the 1970s while recording comedy albums and making film shorts for *Saturday Night Live*. In 1978, Brooks directed his first feature, *Real Life*, a delightful cult classic about a crazed documentary film maker bent on capturing the "true spirit" of a typical American family.

Despite critical raves, *Real Life* disappeared without a trace. "I wanted to start a campaign—'Find *Real Life*,'" Brooks joked. "The first person who could find the theater it was in would win a bumper sticker."

Brooks is more optimistic about *Modern Romance*, which Columbia Pictures says is "doing very well" at the box office in New York and "pretty good" in Los Angeles. "I think I'm going to take Cerritos by surprise," Brooks said. "I can hear them now—who is this man and why is his movie here?"

Brooks is something of an enigma, even to his friends, who sometimes find it difficult to separate the comic from his movie alter ego.

"Albert is very smart, but he's totally obsessive," said Penelope Spheeris, who produced *Real Life*. "He's exactly the same person who ends up on screen. It's as if there's this little demon inside him, saying 'Go, Albert, Go!'

"Like most great comedians, Albert is almost a tragic character. There's a very dark side of him—the humor just covers it over."

Another coworker on one of Brooks's films added: "Albert means well, but he's completely maniacal. It's very difficult working with Albert, because you don't really work *with* him—it's like you don't exist."

The thirty-three-year-old comic shied away from any serious self-appraisals, though he was critical of the way many comics jealously guard their screen personas.

"It's very dangerous to get caught up in the syndrome of protecting your image," he said. "It gets to the point where you're afraid to offend anybody. Gee, maybe I shouldn't drink this glass of water because there's a water shortage.

"You end up not being able to do anything—maybe I should just lie down through the whole picture. I can't make movies that way. You have to take risks and not be afraid to disturb people."

In *Modern Romance*, Brooks takes all those risks—and more. It's easy to embrace the lovable lunacy of Steve Martin and the brainy vanity of Woody Allen, but it's a true act of cinematic courage to ask audiences to sympathize with a dopey, self-absorbed slob who spends most of the picture provoking himself into fits of jealous rage and embarrassment.

Brooks's film is filled with all of the Me Generation's favorite charades, particularly drugs, sexual gamesmanship, and enough banal dialogue to keep a talk show going for a year.

It's no coincidence that Brooks mans the telephone throughout the entire film (even making a call while he's out jogging). The phone is Brooks's perfect satiric weapon—he uses it to make dates with women he barely knows, as well as to fend off prying questions from his mother. ("Call me," she says, "I'll be at the beauty shop." Albert shoots back: "I know the number.")

Brooks is convinced he's merely acting out problems common to any modern romance. "Love and jealousy and anger are universal themes," he said. "People are just lying if they say it doesn't exist. That's why I use the car and the telephone so much in the film. They are to romance what the horse and buggy and the midnight stroll were a hundred years ago."

Because of all the attention he lavishes on neurotic relationships, Brooks often has been compared to Woody Allen. Although they both graduated from stand-up to cinema, Brooks doesn't see much similarity. "He wants to be taken seriously," Brooks argued. "I want to be taken less seriously."

When Brooks attempts to revive his flagging love affair in the film, he leaves a pet giraffe at his girlfriend's door. "If that was Woody Allen," he said, "it would have been a novel."

If Brooks has learned anything from Allen's career, it's the importance of having control over your film. "I don't make movies like *Airplane!*, where if it doesn't work, you can tinker with the jokes. You can't add the fat doctor at the last minute to save the picture.

"Comedy is nuance, which is in the hands of the director. I specialize in underplaying a part. So I don't want to hand the movie over to somebody who's going to smash somebody over the head—if you give the script to Jerry Lewis, you're going to get a different picture."

According to Brooks, directing his own films has helped him mature as an actor. "Most people are impressed by weeping and wailing, but acting really is choices," he said. "The hardest kind of acting is to do *less*. Less is very important. For me, more is a scary word unless you're requesting an Anthony Newley song."

As for *Modern Romance*, Brooks struck a note of cautious optimism. "If success was determined by box-office gross alone, 90 percent of the people in this town would never make a movie again," he noted. "There'll always be room for guys like me. You just keep going until you have a hit, which is usually when you least expect it."

Albert Brooks Is Funnier Than You Think

Paul Slansky / 1983

From *Playboy*, July 1983, 139, 150, 213–18. Reprinted with permission.

It's Thanksgiving Eve in NBC studio 6-A, and Albert Brooks is talking about bowling.

"In every bowling alley, there's a room just a little bit larger than this desk called the pro shop," he tells David Letterman. "It's full of balls and shoes, because that's really all bowling is. Now, there's this guy who works in one in LA—he's a nice guy—and if you listen to him on the phone, he keeps going, '*No problem! No problem!*' What are people saying to him? 'A giant landed from outer space. Do you have a size-95 shoe?' '*No problem!*'"

Brooks pauses for a couple of seconds to experience his favorite earthly noise—the reassuring sound of people laughing at him—and continues. "I started bowling this summer as therapy," he explains. "It's Zenlike. You get to throw this heavy thing as hard as you can at pins. At the alley I go to, you can dress up the pins to look like people you hate."

Albert Brooks has always drawn on his everyday life for his richest comedy, and since he has spent the past seven years in the movie business, most of his jokes tonight are at the expense of the studio heads whose faces he frequently envisions on his bowling pins.

"Columbia put out a picture called *Happy Birthday to Me*," he says. "The ad showed a guy with a skewer through his neck, and there was no such scene in the film. That's a strange kind of advertising. 'What should the ad concept be?' 'How about a skewer through the neck?' 'Great!'"

He switches to another Hollywood topic, video games based on hit movies. "Now it's mandatory," he says. "You go in to present your story idea and the studio people say, 'What's the game in it?' I had an interesting writing assignment. I had to come up with the game for *Ordinary People*—get in the cab and try to get the wife out of town without driving over a pedestrian. And *Norma Rae* was a great video game, where you had to get all these little union dots in one room."

This is Brooks's first TV appearance in almost a year, and he has accumulated a lot of material—so much, in fact, that he's firing off in ten-second bursts the kind of ideas most comics would stretch into ten-minute bits. He moves into dialects, quickly runs through superb impressions of Rudolf Nureyev, Monica Vitti, and Sylvester Stallone, then comes to the star of *Conan the Barbarian*.

"Maybe they'll give Arnold Schwarzenegger a one-man show on cable. He's a good actor," Brooks says, his friendly face radiating sincerity. "He could do, like, *Young F.D.R.*" Brooks slips into Schwarzeneggerese: "Eleanors! I need you upstairs here! De Pearl Harbors is getting all crazy vit de t'ings. Eleanors!" He interrupts this imaginary promo in an announcer's voice—"As young F. D. R., Arnold Schwarzenegger!"—then cuts back to Arnie: "I'll lift up de Russians and t'row dem. Get me de hot phone. I'll skveeze it till it cools down."

Talk-show appearances aren't all that's been keeping Brooks busy during the past few months. His performance with Dan Aykroyd in the upcoming film version of *The Twilight Zone* is in the can, and he is about to costar with Dudley Moore in Howard Zieff's remake of the Preston Sturges comedy *Unfaithfully Yours*. After that, he'd like to begin filming *Lost in America*, a romantic comedy he wrote for ABC Motion Pictures with his friend and longtime collaborator Monica Johnson. Unfortunately, ABC—the studio he told *Variety* he had chosen because it had "an easy name to remember"—rejected the script as not sufficiently commercial, so Brooks is in New York engaging in his least favorite activity: raising money.

Animal House, Nine to Five, and *Smokey and the Bandit* are Hollywood's top-grossing comedies, with combined rentals of more than two hundred million dollars. Brooks's first two films, *Real Life* and *Modern Romance* (both of which he cowrote, directed, and starred in), took in less than five million dollars between them. The fact that Brooks's admirers think he's a genius is irrelevant to the oilmen, real-estate tycoons and soda bottlers who now run the studios. To them, he is merely unbankable. "If, in fact, there were a hell," he says, sitting in his hotel room after the *Letterman* taping, chain-eating pieces of dried fruit, "hell for me would be a place where I'd be given a huge budget and be told to make a movie to please Gene Shalit."

Both of his films had the enthusiastic support of several important critics—Shalit conspicuously *not* among them—and their popularity as pay TV attractions bolsters Brooks's claim that their box-office failures were caused, in part, by the less than wizardly marketing decisions of their distributors. "With *Real Life*, they said they didn't think we needed to advertise on *Mork and Mindy*," he says with the ironic, deadpan delivery that characterizes much of his speech. "I said, 'You're right; why would we need a show that *everybody* watches?' Then the newspaper ads started shrinking to the size of want ads, and when I complained, they said, 'Do you have any *idea* how many people read want ads?'

"When Rex Reed wrote that I had a face like an open-faced sandwich, that was *the* best moment so far," says Brooks. "It's just a thing of mine—I've always wanted to be compared to deli food."

Steve Martin was the guy with the arrow through his head who said, "Excuse me." Chevy Chase smirked and fell down a lot. Cheech and Chong did dope jokes, George Carlin said dirty words, and Andy Kaufman seemed to think that the point of performing was to make people nervous about laughing. For those of us who took comedy seriously in the seventies, though, there was only the holy trinity: Richard Pryor, Lily Tomlin, and Albert Brooks.

Those three can't be summed up in single sentences, and part of our implicit agreement with them is that we encourage them to keep growing. Pryor and Tomlin became superstars, then almost self-destructed, he with his cocaine conflagration and she with her performance in the unspeakably bad *Moment by Moment* (Rex Reed loved it). Brooks has avoided the pitfalls of mass acceptance by avoiding that acceptance. At thirty-five, after sixteen years in the business, he is still not quite a star.

"If you want to know if people come up to me on the street and say, 'Mr. Brooks, I enjoyed your movie even though it was improperly released by the studio,' yes, that happens," Brooks says, several days after the *Letterman* show. He is sipping an iced coffee in a booth in Canter's delicatessen, a Hollywood landmark whose older Jewish clientele has been joined in the past few years by a sizable contingent of punks.

Two of them—a spiky-haired teen in a "FEAR" T-shirt and his barefoot, blonde girlfriend—spot Brooks as they walk past us, toward the bathrooms. Although his six-foot frame is leaner than it appears on camera, he is not difficult to recognize. His unpretentious fashion statement rarely changes: plaid shirt, thin-wale corduroys, and running shoes. His most distinctive feature is his hair, a mass of springy, dark curls that would not be worn by anyone who took himself too seriously. His deep-set eyes and semisad smile combine to form a face that seems both vulnerable and completely honest. It is this honesty that has made Brooks the comic of choice among LA's punk crowd. The kids smile and exchange knowing glances, but they don't stop to talk.

"Basically, I still have the privacy that all celebrities crave," Brooks says, "except for those celebrities who feel that privacy reflects some kind of failure on their part."

Brooks entered the public consciousness in the early seventies with a series of stand-up routines on *The Tonight Show* that are remembered with reverence by

anyone lucky enough to have seen them: the impressionist whose every imita-
tion sounded like Ed Sullivan; the shadow artist with the broken hand who was
reduced to portraying "a bunny hiding behind a rock"; the mime who described
everything he was doing in a French accent ("Now I am walking up ze stairs,
now I am petting ze dog"); and dozens of others. He turned his "Famous School
for Comedians" parody in *Esquire* magazine into a classic film piece on the PBS
series *The Great American Dream Machine.* (The school featured a counselor who
helped students choose the disease in whose honor they wanted to hold telethons.)
His albums, *Comedy Minus One* and *A Star Is Bought,* include such gems as an
audition for a new national anthem ("Got a country, / I spell it A-M-E-R-I-C-A!")
and a version of Ravel's *Bolero* with lyrics ("Hey, is the room just the right temperature? / Should we do it on the couch / Or should we do it on the floor?").

In 1975, *Time* called Brooks "the smartest, most audacious comic since Lenny
Bruce and Woody Allen." Wary of too much success too soon, he was determined
to keep control of his career. He was on the verge of signing to star in *Our Man
in Rattan,* a sitcom about a TV newsman stationed in Africa, when a network
executive asked him, "What do you see for this character in five years?"

"Suicide," Brooks replied, and abandoned the project. He suggested the idea
of rotating guest hosts when he rejected Lorne Michaels's offer to make him the
permanent host of what would become *Saturday Night Live.* He was content not
to do anything unless it was exactly what he wanted to do. That was not a career
strategy designed to land him on the cover of *People,* but it did allow him to create an uncompromised body of work that tends to support those fans—many of
them in the show-business community—who believe that Albert Brooks is the
funniest white man in America.

"Every kid should have an Albert," said his writing partner Monica Johnson a
few years ago. "He's the kind of person you'd want to be locked in jail with. You
know: you don't have a game, you don't have any cigarettes. What could be better
than having Albert Brooks in there?"

Everything sparks Brooks's humor. As we head west on Santa Monica Boulevard in his new car, his associations and references are dazzling. When an Ozzy
Osbourne song comes on the radio, I mention that Osbourne was arrested not
long ago in San Antonio for peeing on the Alamo. "What does a person like that
do when he sells out?" Brooks wonders. "Use a real bathroom?" When a tailgater
gets a little too close, he says, "Cars should come equipped with screens like
that thing in Times Square that spells out the news. Then you could punch out
your own instant messages: WILL THE SMALL RED CAR WITH THE UGLY
DRIVER PLEASE STAY A LITTLE FARTHER BACK?" A squashed dog on the
side of the road elicits the observation, "He might just be taking a nap."

Someone on the radio is talking about Charles Bronson's vigilante movies, *Death Wish* and *Death Wish II*. "I once wrote a vigilante picture," Brooks says, "but it all had to do with killing studio people. You know: they take your parking space back without telling you about it, and then you drive in the next morning and they're raping your wife right in your old spot, and the paint they covered your name with is in her hair. It's hard to sell an idea like that." From there, he *segues* into some thoughts on the cosmic insignificance of movie critics. "How can you take seriously statements like, 'I loved it ten times as much as Rex Reed' or 'Oscar, get into a cab and go to Paul Newman's house. The race is over'? You have to look at a newspaper and see the context in which articles appear. On the front page, there's always the threat of nuclear war. That puts your review in perspective instantly."

Nuclear war is never far from Brooks's mind; as a Jew with an acute awareness of the horror of the Holocaust, he cannot assume that any human activity is unthinkable. I ask him if he has heard White House aide Ed Meese's description of the apocalypse as "something that may not be desirable."

Brooks laughs derisively. "You know," he says, "being president is a lot like making a movie. You write a script—basically, that's your campaign. The studio decides to go ahead—in the president's case, the people elect him. Then they release the movie—in the case of the president, he fires weapons. You never know if a movie's going to appeal to the public, nor do you ever know if weapons will strike key cities. They say that once one nuclear weapon is fired, it could ruin the direction gadgets in all the others. What are the other missiles gonna do? They could turn around and come back at us. It's the same with a movie. Not only could it be a bomb, it could haunt you forever."

When Brooks gets going, his comic momentum seems to take on a life of its own. "The thing that amazed me when I got to know him was his commitment," says comedian Harry Shearer. "Once he decides he's gonna do something—whether it's a movie or a joke—he commits to it totally, which frees him to go as far as he can. Even if it's an idea that just occurred to him that minute, he'll push it as far as possible."

"Albert is like E.T. for adults," Carrie Fisher said recently, describing a weekend boat trip she had taken with Brooks and four other people. "It was like being on a drug that would never end. He never slept and he was never not funny; and, finally, I was scared that he'd follow me everywhere and keep me laughing until I got physically ill and died."

Brooks applies rigorous logic to the absurd world around him and makes material out of whatever doesn't fit—not surprising when you consider that his name at birth was Albert Einstein. (His father, radio comedian Harry Einstein—better known as Parkyakarkus—had resisted the joke with three older sons.)

"I guess I was the class clown," Brooks says, turning the car onto Coldwater Canyon Road for the ride home over the Hollywood Hills to Sherman Oaks. "With a name like Albert Einstein, you don't hide in the back. I would read the school bulletin to the class and I'd add activities and make stuff up. It was good, a good ten minutes every morning."

His father, who had been ill for years, died when Albert was eleven, instilling in him the knowledge that if you waited long enough, the worst would always happen. By then, though, the comics who had hung out at his family's Beverly Hills home knew he was a comedic prodigy. A few years later, when Johnny Carson asked Carl Reiner to name the funniest people he knew, a high school kid named Albert Einstein was near the top of his list. After three years at Carnegie Tech in Pittsburgh, Albert returned to LA, changed his name to avoid cheap laughs, and began his career.

Comedy itself was his favorite subject. His bits—which he often performed on network television without even trying them out on friends—took standard comic formats, such as animal acts or ventriloquists, and made them the butts of his jokes. Increasingly, though, his own life became a source of material. When he couldn't come up with anything new for a scheduled spot on *The Tonight Show*, he went on and did ten of the funniest minutes in TV history about *that*. After explaining to the audience that he'd run out of material earlier in his career than he'd expected, he went through a scornful demonstration of all the things he *could* do if he wanted to settle for lowbrow yoks. Sure, he could get a laugh by dropping his pants, he said, dropping them and getting a big one. Sure, he could amuse people by smashing eggs on his head. Or by drawing a funny face on his chest. Certainly, there were those who'd be convulsed if he mashed a poundcake into his face. At the end, with his pants around his ankles, eggs dripping from his hair, a cake on his face and a face on his chest, he declared, "This isn't the real me." He then pulled an 8″ × 10″ glossy out of his shorts, shouted, "*This* is the real me!" and stalked offstage.

After two years of doing TV, Brooks had built up enough confidence to start performing live. He spent the early seventies headlining in small clubs and opening concerts in larger halls for rock stars like Neil Diamond and Richie Havens. He was miserable. "I never wanted to be a comedian; I wanted to be an actor," he says now. "And I certainly didn't want to be on the road." A tour promoting his first album pushed him over the edge. "When I released that record, I thought, 'Pity those poor salesmen; people are going to be trampling them to get their hands on that album.' That didn't happen. The record wasn't even in the stores."

Six weeks into the tour, he was interviewed by a Boston disc jockey who said to him, "Jonathan Winters went crazy; you think that's ever gonna happen to you?"

"I think it's happening right now," Brooks answered. He canceled the rest of his engagements and flew home.

"What scared me then was that the only thing I had to look forward to was another club," he says. "Also, I think that a lot of times, audiences didn't get things, due to the fact that they didn't see them as fast as they possibly could have, because light was traveling a bit too slow. And now scientists are saying that, in fact, we *aren't* seeing things quite as quickly as they once thought. That hurt my timing. I would do something and there would be that infinitesimal pause, and I would feel crushed. Then there would be that big roar of laughter, but it could never bring me back to where I felt I should be. So, as light speeds up, I plan to go down to the Improv."

Technology is Brooks's abiding passion. As a child, he was one of the first wearers of contact lenses. As a teenager, he listened to electronic music and sound-effects records. As an adult, he is usually one of the earliest owners of such gadgets as a recording Walkman or a wrist-watch video game. He has said that he'd rather spend an afternoon with a surgeon or with someone who works in a jet-propulsion laboratory than with almost anyone in show business.

Today, he's thinking about buying a home computer—he wants to explore the comedic possibilities of those machines—and so we have stopped off at his local computer center. Brooks wanders through the store playing with them. He punches some numbers into a talking computer, then says, "How much does Redford want for *E. T. II*?"

"THIRTY-EIGHT-MILLION-SIX-HUNDRED-NINETY-TWO-THOUSAND-THREE-HUNDRED-FIFTY-FOUR," the computer fires back.

We overhear a cashier telling a customer that the store will be open on New Year's Day. "These people don't have regular holidays," Brooks says. "They celebrate Binary Day in November—the tenth."

After experimenting for twenty minutes, he is tempted to buy an Apple II on the spot. This is the first place he's looked, though, and he's not sure whether or not they're cheaper someplace else. "Are these good prices?" he asks one of the teenaged technobrats behind the counter.

The kid nods. "Sometimes, we have even bigger sales and lower prices."

"For instance, when?" Brooks asks.

"Oh, just sometimes," the kid says.

"Yes, but *when*?" Brooks persists. "Tell me. You think it might be any minute now? Should I wait outside?"

The kid can't tell if Brooks is kidding. Without a hint of irony, he answers, "No."

People often don't know how to take Brooks, and he has not made it easy for them. *Super Season* (one of six short films he made for the first season of *Saturday Night Live*) was intended as a savage parody of prime-time TV, but it featured promos for shows so accurately inane—*Black Vet* (a Black Vietnam veteran takes up practice as a veterinarian in a small Southern town), *Medical Season*, and *The Three of Us*—that the last, a sitcom about a young man living with two women, actually turned up on Fred Silverman's prime-time ABC schedule two years later as *Three's Company*.

In his first film, *Real Life*, Brooks played an egomaniacal comedian who set out to film an entire year in the lives of a typical American family and almost destroyed the family in the process. (To further blur the line between fantasy and reality, the comic was named Albert Brooks.) In *Modern Romance*, he played a jealous lover so obsessed by his unworkable relationship that he tried to trace his girlfriend's long-distance phone calls in an effort to prove her suspected infidelity. Many moviegoers walked out of theaters hating his characters. (Brooks has also played memorable nerds in his two other film appearances: he was Cybill Shepherd's pompous campaign coworker in *Taxi Driver*, and, as a horny bridegroom in *Private Benjamin*, he died during sex with Goldie Hawn in the movie's opening minutes.)

"All I'm saying is that it's OK to present yourself as you are," Brooks says when he's back in the car. "I think I present a different side of a male character, a side that is not John Wayne–like, a side that is, in fact, destructible. To some people, that is refreshing, and to other people, especially if they don't know me, it may be disturbing.

"I don't see many explosions or ten-car crashes in the course of my life," he continues, "so I don't put them into my movies. I would love to live in a society where *My Dinner with Andre* made one hundred million dollars. Then I would be in the mainstream. I could do that stuff easier than I could do *Meatballs*. It would be terrible if I tried to make *Meatballs*, lost my mind doing it, and people loved it. Then what would I do? They'd want more, and I'd have to go back into my insanity to get more."

He pulls into the driveway of an unpretentious one-story house and parks under an orange tree. "If you don't succeed on your own ground, then there's no reason to succeed," he says. "Unless, of course, you really want a boat. If you're a person who feels that with a yacht, everything will be all right, then you should do whatever you have to and get the yacht."

Brooks doesn't need the yacht; he lives in the Valley "because it's cheaper than Beverly Hills." Each room of his sparsely furnished home is dominated by electronic equipment. The living room features a projection TV, the sitting room houses a pair of four-foot-tall speakers, and the bedroom contains another large-screen TV, a video-cassette recorder, a video-game system, and an exercise bike that provides a digital readout of your pulse. (Although he gets little exercise aside from bowling and sex, Brooks is extremely health-conscious: he doesn't smoke cigarettes, drinks only sake, eats no red meat, and takes massive quantities of vitamins.)

He has been linked with several beautiful women, among them Linda Ronstadt (they lived together), Candice Bergen, and his *Modern Romance* costar, Kathryn Harrold. He is currently between serious relationships, and he refuses to talk publicly about his love life. "I just think that I don't have to discuss the women I sleep with with the vendor I buy *Playboy* from," he says, tossing the day's mail onto the kitchen table. "When a guy says to me, 'Heeey! Is she as good as she looks?' then I draw the line."

We go into the den—obviously a room in which he spends a lot of time. On the bookshelves is a complete bound set of his father's radio scripts. The brown carpet is covered by a mass of tangled wires leading to the sound system in the closet. Cassettes and their empty plastic cases are everywhere. I remove two piles of papers and magazines from the couch, and we sit down to talk about the movie business.

Brooks thinks he may have a backer for his new film, though he may be forced to keep the budget to a minuscule three million dollars. "I can make it for whatever amount they say," he explains. "The size of the budget translates directly into how much time I have to sleep while I'm working. On three million dollars, I'll get about an hour a night."

I bring up Woody Allen, with whom Brooks is often compared and whom he greatly admires. How has Allen's recent dry spell at the box office affected Hollywood's attitude toward intelligent screen comedies? "The reason Woody was able to keep making films when he was starting out was that the studios were solid," Brooks says. "People did not have the fear of losing their jobs if a mistake was made, which began to happen when the conglomerates took over.

"*Stardust Memories*, which I love, took in less than four million dollars. If Woody hadn't had a reputation, he'd be out. And it was tougher for me after that flopped, because I could no longer say, 'Look at Woody!' I was pitching my movie to the man who had backed his least profitable picture, and the advice I got before I went in was, 'By the way, don't use Woody in this meeting, because they lost a great deal of money on his last film.'"

To Brooks, the most contemptible aspect of corporate Hollywood is the craven reliance on research. "Anything that confirms their research kills art," he declares. "I'm positive that every bit of research told them, 'Make *Annie*.' Research has been refined to such a degree that the movie does not even have to be viewed.

"To me, *Annie* is ten five-million-dollar pictures. When I was in school, movies were still the place where new things seemed to be encouraged. Not anymore. I heard Ray Stark or someone like him on a radio talk show while I was driving. 'What about creativity?' the interviewer asked him, and he said, 'Creativity doesn't sell at this point.' It's true. You go to a studio head and say, 'I've got the greatest new idea,' and he says, 'Olden it up and come back.'

"One of the stupidest statements in this business is 'The public likes it.' Well, maybe people would like something else, *if* they got to see it. Lake Michigan is nice—until you see Acapulco. Ten years ago, the studio heads thought audiences were sheep," Brooks says. "Now they think they're snails with Down's syndrome."

Lately, Brooks has been feeling the need for feedback from audiences rather than from studio heads. In October, he went to Phoenix and had the best time he's had in years, substituting for a week as the host of a local morning radio show. He gets up now, pops a cassette into his machine, and plays a segment in which children call in and talk about their video-game dreams.

"Do you play the game a lot?" Brooks asked a little girl whose recurring nightmare had her being chased by the gorilla from *Donkey Kong*.

"Yes," she said.

"Do you want to stop dreaming about it?" Brooks asked.

"Yes," she said.

"Stop playing it, honey," Brooks advised.

He gets up again and runs the tape forward to find other highlights, including "Wake Up a Star" (in which he placed an on-the-air call to his friend Rob Reiner at seven a.m.) and, thanks to the brilliant impression work of Harry Shearer, a pair of phone interviews with President Reagan. The radio experience was so positive, he says, that he is thinking about doing some live performing. "All along, I've been telling myself that if I got out in the clubs after all these years and performed live, that would be my trump card. Well, I may not be that popular. Whatever; I'm getting ready to take the consequences either way.

"When I was doing stand-up," he continues, "I noticed that the same bits that got blank stares when I first did them got huge laughs later in my career. Well, I didn't choose to stop doing them. I think it's a combination of the audience and the performer getting used to each other. You change a little, they accept a bit more. The business tries to get you to change completely. People tell you, 'Obviously, you're doing something wrong; you did not make one hundred million dollars. Go back, rethink your birth, and come back to us like everyone else.' That's the trap of making comedy on a commercial basis: if you don't sell enough of it, you are branded a failure. So you try to please the studio *and* the audience *and* still keep enough integrity to allow you to sleep. As you get older, you need less and less integrity to sleep—or you just stay awake. That's why they have twenty-four-hour cable services."

He pauses for a beat, then goes on. "I enjoy making three people laugh as much as I enjoy making three million people laugh. It's just that, businesswise, three is not quite as impressive a number to a large studio. 'Three, huh? So we're guaranteed fifteen dollars at evening prices? It's a go!'

"To me, the satisfaction is not in numbers. It's that I'm making sense to other living human beings. It's instant confirmation that I *am* from this planet and that I deserve to continue living here.

"I'm in this for the whole fight," says Brooks. "I'm going to stick it out and try to do it. I guess I've stopped having expectations because they don't seem to be realized when I think they will, which leads me to believe that they'll be realized when I *least* expect it. So I'm trying to least expect it right now."

Seriously, Here's Albert Brooks

David Elliott / 1985

From the *San Diego Union*, April 7, 1985, E-1, E-8. Used with permission from the *San Diego Union-Tribune*. Copyright 2015 the *San Diego Union-Tribune*, LLC. All rights reserved.

Albert Brooks was born Albert Einstein, and is still a brain. His film comedies—the latest, most elegant, and probably most popular is *Lost in America*—win laughs intelligently. They don't grab and squeeze, like a salesman with a joy buzzer.

"Many people tend to hear 'comedy' and think 'stupid,'" he notes, more bemused than amused. "When I was nineteen years old, people would ask what I did. I said I do comedy and they said, 'Great, when are you going to Vegas?' I'd say, 'No, I'm not going to Vegas. I just do comedy.'"

In *Lost in America* he does comedy and also gets to Vegas. Brooks plays David Howard, a rising star of the LA ad biz who doesn't get a promised promotion. He crashes out of the fast track with his wife Linda (Julie Hagerty), who also dumps her job, and they set off in a huge camper to "touch an Indian" in deepest America. In Las Vegas, they find no Indian, but David's control fetish is scalped as Linda discovers the giddy release of high-stakes gambling. David touches desperation.

If it's a road comedy, it isn't *Cannonball Run*. Sitting in his dark, bare office at the Warners Hollywood studio, a space adorned only with hopes that his third film as director may be his first hit ("We broke the house record in Chicago"), Brooks takes rightful pride in the fact that David and Linda "go out on the road and don't get into car crashes. We had a preview in Seattle and I saved two cards that I thought were great. One said, 'Too real to be a comedy.' The other said, 'This happened to me!'

"I then said to Warners, 'Name one comedy in the last two years that can be said about. At least give me credit for that!' I mean, it's not *National Lampoon's Vacation*. Who's gonna say, 'Sure, this happened to me, my wheels all fell off, we taped my dead grandmother to the roof, and then we made it to an amusement park that closed for the summer'?"

What's real in movieland is that Brooks, hailed by *Playboy* (no less) as "the funniest white man in America," has had to scramble. Relating the tale, he works himself into a propulsive spin that is both funny and bottom-line serious:

"It's not easy to move from movie to movie, without some profit. With *Real Life*, which was an independent effort, it took me a year and a half to raise half a million dollars. Then Columbia let me make *Modern Romance*, which was not a smash hit. This film I wrote for ABC Pictures, then they got started, and then they kind of figured out they would make *National Lampoon's Reunion* instead. That left me out on the trail, and there's nothing much worse. You spend a year of your life, unpaid, and then you're flying to New York to talk to small companies which say 'Yes' and then you don't hear from them for three months."

So you were lost in America?

"Literally."

Fortune, in the form of producer David Geffen, stepped in. The film was made, with class but no frills. Then it was released February 15 "in one Manhattan theater and about eleven in New Jersey, during this incredible onslaught of movies. Well, I can't keep up with *Turk 182* in Paramus. There's no graffiti in my movie!

"So then the studio people think, 'Uh oh, New Jersey doesn't like it.' Which is sort of silly, as usual, because New Jersey doesn't really know about it. But it does well in Manhattan, then Chicago, and Boston is great, and all of a sudden they're thinking, 'Gee, look at this picture.' That's the way this business works, or doesn't work. But if my film had come out fast, all over, we wouldn't be here now talking."

Career fretting is no laughing matter, but it plays right into Brooks's comic image as High Anxiety Jr., the brainy, speed-talking mensch who is definitely not macho. His favorite of his works is *Modern Romance*, in which his character went wiggy over young love, "because I think it's gutsy to present a male like that. Women liked it more than most men, because I think the guy made men uncomfortable. It takes a long time to wear the John Wayne image down, to show that men can be something less than monolithic."

The inevitable comparison is to Woody Allen, of whom Brooks says, "Thank goodness he's out there, doing something against the grain. But look at his character, he's someone you can feel sorry for, like the Little Tramp. Me, I'm not a small man and I can't play for much sympathy. If I get beat up, people think, 'What's your problem here?' Most movie comedy features characters you can feel blatantly sorry for. I love Laurel and Hardy, but those guys are pitiful characters. Or the Three Stooges. They get punched around, you gonna say, 'Hell, you guys got it made. What's your problem?'

"One card I saved from the *Modern Romance* preview, because the studio made a real point of showing it to me, was 'He's got a good-looking girlfriend, and a nice car, what's his problem?' I really couldn't answer that. But I'm saying that maybe the modern comic problem isn't that obvious, it's not 'Here's a 90,000-pound guy with no girl and no job.' It's 'You can have a good job and wife and still have a problem.' Most people do!"

David and Linda, in *Lost in America*, find that their problem is not to find an Indian to touch. It's to make changes that finally lead back to liking who they are. The movie's ending is abrupt, a little startling, and free of cant.

Brooks smiles as he notes, "It takes courage to say, 'We've made a mistake. Let's correct it before it's too late.' Some people say, 'We would have stayed out there in the country,' and I think, 'Would you? And do what? Go trout fishing in Arizona? Besides, it takes some real money to support that Winnebago.' . . . Most movies pretend money doesn't exist. People in them live on love, and freedom, and weather, all those things I've never been able to live on. When I was seventeen I was in love, sure, but I still had to buy my date dinner! And when you get older, it gets even worse."

As for the finish, which some viewers see as a rush for the exit, he is "proud of it because it gets a great laugh yet is very realistic. . . . It's happy but not traditional. It's one of the reasons I wanted to make this film, because it's correct. It wouldn't be correct for David to take three more school crossing-guard jobs, in order to find himself."

The film is a visible advance in art for Brooks, whose fine wit and timing are matched by Eric Saarinen's razor-crisp photography. It's the first Brooks comedy to have a Woody Allen sheen, but with precise restraint, as he explains: "Eric and I had a phrase while we were shooting: 'real beautiful.' As opposed to 'real beautiful.' To err towards prettiness, a bit, but present things so you feel you are just there, watching. . . . Yet after my other movies I don't want to be punished again for making things so real people thought it was a news program."

Getting back to the news, will *Lost* be a hit, and give Albert Brooks the career he deserves? He is hopeful but not exactly sanguine: "If my film's a success it helps me, maybe, make another movie, but as a friend of mine said recently, 'We don't live in a time when studios say, "That was a great movie, let's make another one."' As it all becomes a huge corporate business, things get so safe. There are too many computers in place to make show business a nonrisk business. Is there anything less creative than a sequel? Sure, there was *Godfather, Part II*, but what about all the others? I thought cable might pick up the slack, but the programming has been so disappointing. I took something to HBO and they said, 'It's too far out.' I said, 'Far out? How far out can it be, when you have it wired into people's homes? They'll watch it!'"

He feels the film biz has "gotten ridiculous. You know, some critics around the country are like my pals now. A few weeks ago I got a call from Michael

Blowen of the *Boston Globe*. He said, 'Albert, I'm ready to quit. You know what film did the best in Boston today? *The Mutilator!*' Then he called back after my film opened and said, 'Thank you. I can keep going.' So even if it can be proven most filmgoers are under twenty, look, I know some sixteen-year-olds, and they're smarter than adults think."

On a roll of analytic indignation, Brooks touches the sixteen-year-old Albert Einstein within and comes up with—the Cheese Analogy. "It's like, say you eat Velveeta and like it. And I give you some fine Swiss cheese that's a little tart. The first time you'll probably say, 'Yecch,' but maybe by the third or fourth time you'll like it, and your brain will figure out, 'Gee, the tartness is what makes it better.' It's the same with art, but if kids aren't given any better, how can they reject *Porky's Revenge*? So the studios turn around and say—this is my least favorite argument—'They're buying, so give them what they like.'"

And comedy, which to be good has to be lifted out of the air by its transparent wings, is the hardest to make fly in the modern market (and never mind Eddie Murphy). We are talking the day after the Academy Awards, and I mention to Brooks Steve Martin's wistful backstage remark, "Maybe I'll always be a dress extra at the Oscars." Brooks is sympathetic but not surprised: "I frankly think Martin was not prejudiced against. It's comedy in general. . . . I went to Carnegie Tech, a good acting school, but the people others thought were the best actors were always those that yelled and cried. If you made tears come out of your face, you got an A, if you also screamed you got an A-plus. If you play blind, or deformed, you win Oscars. We could handicap the awards for the next ten years by looking at the scripts that have good sad, crippled roles. It goes to a gut feeling in people that if you laugh it's silly, not serious."

But seriously, folks, Albert (Einstein) Brooks may finally be on the verge of being more than a cult success. He wouldn't mind simply starring in someone else's movie ("If I were willing to play spies I could get Chevy Chase roles") but until something juicy comes along, no doubt both serious and funny, he will continue to write, direct, act, and shake down the deals . . .

"I'd really like to be home at seven and let somebody else argue with the studio all night. But so far, I have to do it all in order to do anything at all I really want to do."

Real Afterlife

Robert DiMatteo / 1991

From *Film Comment*, March 1991, 18–24. Reprinted with permission from *Film Comment* and the Film Society of Lincoln Center. © *Film Comment* 1991.

Brainy and brash, the deadpan satirist of the movies, Albert Brooks goes it alone. From *Real Life* to the current *Defending Your Life*, he has dragged himself through his movies, looking a little pained and discombobulated. "Where's the party?" he seems to be wondering; "I didn't get invited." If you're an outsider type who tends to think the world is bonkers, Brooks is like an old friend. He confirms your fears, he makes you giggle.

Speaking of fears, there's the tonic *Defending Your Life*. As always, Brooks stars, this time playing Daniel, an anxiety-fraught advertising exec who is killed in a car accident because, miming to Barbra Streisand's "Something's Coming," he has dipped below the dashboard of his moving car to retrieve some errant CDs. When he wakes up, the poor schlump finds himself in a gleaming modern Shangri-La—a vacation resort of self-discovery known as Judgment City. The place is designed to minimize apprehension, so that those who have been sent there can confront and work through their fears. Werner Erhard couldn't come up with a better utopia. To facilitate self-exploration, everything has been made perfect, including breakfast, which is the same fabulous eggs-bacon-toast-fruit-and-juice delight each morning—and you don't have to worry about weight gain. The temperature in Judgement City is seventy-four degrees every day and, as the Weather Channel proclaims, it's "perfectly clear all the time." Go to the Past Lives Pavilion and you'll be greeted by your own hologram of Shirley MacLaine.

Each day, Daniel meets with the tribunal that will judge his progress and determine whether he should be sent back to Earth for another go-around or promoted to a higher sphere. One day he meets Julia, a beautiful fellow novitiate who is clearly more evolved than he. (With her lustrous blond hair, long classical nose, and gentle, knowing smile, Meryl Streep looks ready for immortality.) She's clearly destined to move on to the next level, her psychic business satisfactorily concluded. Daniel wants to go too.

Obviously, there's a dippiness built into this material. Moralism hovers over it as well. If Brooks's tone weren't so light and playful, the film might collapse. And the writer-director does run out of steam around two-thirds of the way through. But if his conceptualization has its limitations, it's also amazing how far Brooks's detached humor can carry him. Afterward, when you think back over the film, you may find yourself marveling at his jest—at the way he both mocks and extols the concept of self-discovery. At the same time, the movie dabbles in spirituality and the afterlife. Even with a finish that can only be called upbeat, the film never makes you squirm.

Throughout his career, Albert Brooks has toyed with an understated form of absurdism. Some first remember him from *The Tonight Show*, where he did comedy bits like the one involving an impressionist whose impersonations all tended to sound like Ed Sullivan. Others treasure his film and TV parodies for *Saturday Night Live* (especially an uncanny, and at the time incredible, prediction of *Three's Company*). His first feature, *Real Life* (1979), was a sharp and droll sendup of the PBS series *An American Family* and the (often nonsensical) cinéma-vérité movement of documentary filmmaking. Charles Grodin, the actor who probably comes closest to matching Brooks's deadpan, starred as a veterinarian whose household was chosen for on-camera scrutiny. While mocking the methodology of the social scientists conducting this experiment, *Real Life* entertained a serious agenda concerning the need for privacy in a society where just about the only thing that is still private is property.

Modern Romance, Brooks's 1981 comedy, opened to mixed reviews, though some of us have a special affection for it. What seemed to throw people was the wavering tone: the behavior of the protagonist alternated between sympathetic and offensive. Never one to romanticize the characters he plays, Brooks stayed true to his role—Robert Cole, a neurotic film editor who can't manage a relationship with his girlfriend (Kathryn Harrold), though he's completely preoccupied with her. Rambling and marked by long takes, the movie stands out from Brooks's other work. It can be annoying, partly because the characters themselves are annoying. But it touches an emotional chord rare in satirical comedy; it's like a more melancholy, harder-edged *Annie Hall*.

The connection between Woody Allen and Brooks—the premier comic auteurs of contemporary American film—is fruitful to consider. They're both Jewish but Brooks, being from a later generation, doesn't seem to have had his humor formed so thoroughly on the analyst's couch. He's almost postanalytic, if you will. Nor does Brooks's Jewishness seem as crucial to his comic vision—whereas Allen can't let the subject alone. It may be relevant to mention here that Brooks hails from Los Angeles, and doesn't have the same degree of cultural "Jewish" angst that we associate with Woody Allen's New York. What the two men share, though, is a wry intelligence and a bravery in being self-deprecating.

One of the great scenes in *Modern Romance* follows Robert around his apartment as he talks on the phone and stumbles this way and that, often talking to himself. He's drunk and on 'ludes, and the scene builds to his getting into his car—and falling asleep! The camera is stationary; the quality of the light changes, and we realize it's morning. Robert wakes up and goes inside. Somehow, the scene has a sad existential quality: it even reminded me a little of a moment in Polanski's *Knife in the Water*, which also pivots on the car as an emblem of aloneness. Of course, Brooks has us laughing a few seconds later. His mixture of moods keeps us on our toes.

Brooks does some of his strongest dramatic acting in this movie. As written by him and his frequent collaborator Monica Johnson, Robert is forlorn, wracked by romantic confusion. He's more isolated that the Woody Allen protagonists in *Annie Hall* and *Hannah and Her Sisters*—more susceptible to self-destructiveness and rage. And he still cracks you up. Brooks is to be commended for avoiding the easy solution, an explosion of craziness to resolve Robert's frustration. The movie limns a unique portrait of masculine vulnerability.

Lost in America (1985) is Brooks's most popular movie to date. It came out right in the middle of the Reagan era, when yuppie consumerism was as at high tide, and Brooks's onslaught is full-bore. He and Julie Hagerty play David and Linda, a prospering married couple who have just put down a $450,000 deposit on a house. Everything seems to be going well, but for one problem: David has a real temper and doesn't know when to chill out. When his boss gives him a promotion he doesn't want, he has a fit, and soon he's been fired. Impulsively, he hurries over to Linda's office and tells her to quit her job, too. Before you can say "drop out," they take to the road in a shiny new thirty-foot Winnebago, and Brooks's yup version of *Easy Rider* is in place.

It's a dandy idea, ingeniously handled. There are plot developments that feel true, and yet are miracles of quirkiness. While staying in Vegas, David goes to bed one night only to wake to find Linda missing. She's been down in the casino and she's blown their life savings. After all these years together, David never knew that Linda had a gambling problem. It hadn't come up before.

Later, bereft of money, Linda gets a job in a fast-food place, and she tells David about her supervisor. We picture a boss. One day the supervisor knocks at the door of their Winnebago and he's about sixteen years old. Brooks's double-takes here are priceless. And Julie Hagerty is the perfect innocent who's hard to stay mad at. For a small-scale film, *Lost in America* careens all over the place—a Winnebago-ride of a movie. Brooks holds it all together, as much with his dry, sneaky acting as with what he does behind the camera. That's true of all his pictures. It's also true of movies like *Broadcast News* and the remake of *Unfaithfully Yours*, where he loans himself out as an actor. His acting and directing are perfect extensions of one another: no one can represent and redeem obnoxiousness the way he can. I think one reason some of us love him so much is that we know he won't get gooey.

He comes close, though, in *Defending Your Life*. It's hard to believe it, but this brilliant cynic in his early forties seems to be casting around for a value system—for something to believe in. With its bright, clean Ida Random (*Silverado, Rain Man, War of the Roses*) production design and its Allen Daviau (*E.T.*) cinematography, the movie looks at times like a Spielberg fantasy. For the first time, Brooks seems willing to forsake irony for whimsy. Mostly, though, *Defending Your Life* is a charming comedy of self-realization.

I interviewed Albert Brooks in 1979 for a San Francisco FM radio show, so it was fun to come back to him now. In many ways, he's the same fellow—loquacious, feisty, a little spacey. He has a peculiar detachment: sometimes he talks about his films as if he himself didn't make them—as if they're somebody else's, and he's trying to figure them out along with the rest of us.

Robert DiMatteo: *Lost in America* was your biggest success. Has it made much money in this country?

Albert Brooks: Are you in the same country? What country are you in? I think it did fine, it didn't cost very much, and it played around for a while. I know it did well on cassette. And when I see the Warners people they smile at me, so I don't think I've hurt anybody.

RD: By making money, I meant something more akin to *Pretty Woman*. Did you see that?

AB: Yes, I did. I am not going to comment about another movie during the precious few words of my interview. [*This from a man who spent the last half of his interview talking about the war in the Middle East.*] Let's talk about something more constructive.

RD: All right. How about Purgatory?

AB: Yeah!

RD: What I take, anyway, to be your version of Purgatory in *Defending Your Life*: Judgment City. Isn't that a fairly Catholic concept for a Jewish boy?

AB: One thing that makes it not religious at all in my mind is that it's not Purgatory based on good or bad, it's whether you have accomplished what you wanted to in life. And I don't think that's particularly a religion, not religion like I have always heard of.

In traditional religion it's like, you know if you're bad you'll go to Hell. This place says if you are chicken you will go back [to Earth]. So a) there's no hell, and b) it's the idea of repeating until you get it right, which I think is a nonreligious idea. I don't think there is any concept of sin in Judgment City. There are hints of it, which I like. I love it when Rip Torn [terrific as Daniel's advocate] says, "Did you give a lot to charity?" "What do you mean, 'a lot'?" And he says, "I'm just asking. Just interested." But it's not the way the judgment seems to be determined.

RD: It looks like a great place to go on holiday—especially if you're worn out from New York or LA. How did you get the visual concept of Judgment City?

AB: Ida Random and Allen Daviau worked on it, and [the special-effects people] helped. The look was really designed, it was thought about carefully. I really tried to figure out: if you were running the place, how would you best do it? I decided you'd want to make it comfortable for people, and I thought that the way to make it most comfortable is to make it familiar. So the word "familiar" was the guideline. Remember when the woman says that they're putting in six mini-malls just outside of town? That's part of the familiarity, constantly updating.

The only things I have ever seen in motion pictures about death focus on all that angelic stuff—the wings and the clouds. Like Peggy Lee, I kept thinking, "Is that all there is?" Then, like Peggy Lee, I thought maybe I should have gotten a larger popcorn. You know, there must be something else, and I've been thinking about it over the years.

RD: I've been losing friends right and left to AIDS and other things. I wondered if some personal death-related experiences have put the subject of the afterlife in your mind.

AB: Well, my father died when I was eleven years old, so I probably got a head start on it. I got some extra years thinking, gee, where did Dad go? And I never liked the concept of heaven and hell—it was so black and white.

One afternoon I thought to myself, "Well, did we make all of this up?" Maybe the universe runs a little bit like a corporation, like IBM. Maybe not, but there is certainly a shot that it does. What if the afterlife is a progression, almost like a promotion, but not necessarily a promotion for do-gooders, but for people who could take care of themselves? If human beings were to be anything more than this you'd want to make sure they were functioning, and it would be almost, like, you know, before you could solo in an airplane you gotta go land in that simulator.

So I focused on fear for the movie. (I'm actually explaining this like I never did before. Make a note of it.) The only thing that seems to bind us all is that we're afraid of something. Human beings are scared, we run into bomb shelters, we hide, and we all share that. In my own life, I am always trying to deal with the things that make me nervous.

RD: Yet, curiously, your film is very upbeat.

AB: I guess it is. Believe me, I didn't set out to make an optimistic movie—having dropped out in one movie and losing my girl in another. I guess in some fundamental way I believe there is a better place to be than here.

RD: At the end, Daniel and Julia pass into another state. Where are they going?

AB: I didn't think that far. I'll think about it, I'll probably think about it. I know what Rip Torn's character says to me initially, that there are many more exciting destinations for smarter people who are not afraid. I would assume, for example, that killing for peace is something that humans would grow out of.

RD: The use of Meryl Streep was kind of inspired. Was it a big deal to work with her?

AB: I was introduced to her socially at a dinner and we talked, and she was very nice and complimentary, and mentioned that it would be fun to do something together.

RD: Magic words?

AB: Yeah, no, just a person who has an interest in working with someone. I must say, I don't think I would have approached her had I not had that opportunity. She had just done *Postcards [from the Edge]* and it was great. We hit it off, and you find out instantly that Meryl is funny. And there's a quality she has in this movie that I think is a bit different from her other stuff.

RD: Each time she shows up in the film, she has this beaming quality, and . . .

AB: You want to be with her.

RD: She really doesn't have that much screentime, does she?

AB: Well, I wasn't in *Broadcast News* that much, but I felt that it was an important character. You can have people in a movie who never leave the screen, and on the way home in the car you don't even remember them. I was a big fan of Meryl's before this movie but, you know, when you become a movie star, projects begin with the person, and then movies are built around you. Whereas on this movie, Meryl really was a team player.

RD: Watching her in *Postcards from the Edge*, I got the idea that she was tired of everybody talking about the accents and the serious characters, and that she wanted to do something different. *Defending Your Life* is a continuation of that.

AB: When Meryl came on the scene in the late seventies, she was so good that she blew people away, and they just kept giving her awards. So that in about ten years, she got what an average person would get in a lifetime. Now, no matter how good you are, after a while people will ask, "What else is new? I don't want to hear another accent!" So Meryl is smart to go and nuke her image.

RD: Do you like merely acting in a movie?

AB: Absolutely. It gives me extraordinary pleasure not to have to look at the circles under my eyes from only getting one hour of sleep. You know, put a bag there or I won't watch.

RD: In your acting there's an Albert Brooks persona the way there's a Woody Allen one.

AB: Yes, though that doesn't mean that the persona isn't worked on or modified. I am sure that in real life, when Jack Benny's friends said something, he didn't look off to the right, with his hand up like that.

RD: I think there's a special pleasure we get from renewing a friendship with a comic actor in film after film. I missed Woody Allen in *Alice*; I found myself thinking that he had Mia Farrow sounding like him. But I wanted him.

AB: I think those vocal rhythms come from working with somebody so often.

RD: I watched *Modern Romance* on tape the other night, and thought of Cassavetes. Is that a meaningful association?

AB: No. I think Cassavetes did some amazing things, but I don't like the feeling of ad-libbing while the camera is rolling.

RD: End of subject. How do you feel about *Defending Your Life*?

AB: It's the movie I most want people to see. As a society, we need lots of new thought.

RD: Do you believe that people should be accountable for their actions? Your film would seem to say so.

AB: Yes, I do. The word "selfish" has gotten a very bum rap. All the Me Generation suggested to people was "Screw you, I'm driving my BMW." But there is another side: if I go inside my house and figure out what kind of human being I want to be, then life is going to be better because of me. It's the only way things are really helped. You can have a thousand Saddam Husseins and a thousand Red Crosses to patch up what he does, and you are always going to have the same kind of world problems. But if you can figure things out, so that you don't walk around feeling like some insecure jerk all day, then maybe you won't treat people that way. For what it's worth, I can't imagine that anybody who chops people's hands off has a good sex life.

Albert Brooks

Bill Zehme / 1991

Hello and welcome. You have begun to read something we like to call the Albert Brooks Celebrity Profile. This is an exciting opportunity for you to learn about Albert Brooks, a man most experts believe to be the funniest human being currently living. You say, If Albert Brooks is so funny, why haven't I seen more of him? The answer is not simple, but let me ask you this: Is it necessary to see more of someone in order to appreciate how funny he or she is? In fact, aren't most people actually funnier in retrospect than they are when you're with them? And what's funny, anyway? It's a foolish word, when you think about it. *Funny*. How would *you* like to be called "funny"? It's not exactly dignified, is it? Therefore, if people were running around calling you the *funniest man alive*, maybe you wouldn't want to be making a public spectacle of yourself. Maybe you'd like a little privacy and prefer to stay at home and watch a great deal of television and think about death. Well, that's what comedian-auteur Albert Brooks has done, and now he's ready to talk about it—just in time to coincide with the release of his fourth film in twelve years, *Defending Your Life*, in which he and Meryl Streep portray two very funny dead people.

Long ago, when life cost less, Albert Brooks roamed the earth. He had curly hair then, and his posture was rigid. Also, he wore much plaid. Even so, he was merciless. If he came upon houses, he would bring them down. If he came upon aisles, he would force people to roll in them. The great hosts of television—Sullivan, Griffin, Carson—loosed him upon their viewing herds, and always he left them laughing. They laughed when he left, you see, because if he had stayed, audience members might have died or possibly suffered internal bleeding. Years later he would say, "My biggest fear was of being *too* funny and murdering people by making them cough and winding up in a lawsuit."

36

And so he stopped.

He turned to film—not literally, of course, but as a career move. No longer would he speak before mobs or visit men with microphones on their desks. Immediacy bored him; he craved *delayed* response. He wondered, "If I created a humorous concept today, would people laugh when they experienced it a *year* from now? What about *three* years?" The challenge was irresistible. First he made six short films that aired on *Saturday Night Live*, a brand-new program for which he declined an offer to be the permanent host. (Such was his comic enormity.) In one film, Israel and Georgia traded places. In another, Albert ordered in roasted chicken. Then, in 1979, Paramount released his first feature, *Real Life*, an echo of the classic PBS documentary *An American Family*, in which he portrayed a comedian named Albert Brooks who spent months filming daily tedium in a Phoenix household until, desperate for action, he set it aflame. Two years later he unveiled *Modern Romance*, perhaps the finest film ever made about horrible behavior in love. In 1985, his third film, *Lost in America*, about a couple who give up everything to live in a Winnebago, succeeded in a way its predecessors did not: many people saw it. But never was he more visible than in *Broadcast News*, the 1987 movie made not by Albert Brooks but by his friend James L. Brooks, in which Albert delivered an Oscar-nominated performance as a brilliant network correspondent who sweats prodigiously on-camera. (From *The Larry King Show*, on radio, last summer. Caller: "How did you get all that sweat to pour from your head?" Albert [*in a rare media appearance*]: "They read me the back-end deal that I made.")

In between all of the others, he was nowhere to be found, unless you went over to his house.

Albert Brooks Reinvents Comedy

Albert: Knock, knock.
You: Who's there?
Albert: [*Pauses, confused*] I don't know—what do you mean?

I have never been to Albert Brooks's house, and he has never been to mine. And yet, we have both been to other people's homes. He is rigorously private and difficult to pin down without the help of several muscular men. Like many private persons, he has much to protect. One day, for instance, I ask him on the telephone to describe the contents of his refrigerator, since there would be no chance of me seeing for myself. He goes to look, then reports:

"Chopped-up fruit. Melon and cantaloupe. Spinach in a bag, which, by the way, is a great delicacy. Nonfat milk. Six truffles, a layer cake, a wedding cake and a human body."

He is known as Comedy's Recluse. Imprisoned by impossibly high standards, he has become a show-business hermit. He is uncompromised, therefore unseen. As such, he lives a hermit's life, if hermits lived in the San Fernando Valley, had offices at Warners, drove Mercedes, ate great quantities of sushi, and thrilled to the company of beautiful women. For the most part, however, he burrows in the handsome Sherman Oaks ranch home where he has dwelled for nine years. There, he will phone up friends and disguise his voice, pretending to be an angry neighbor or a law-enforcement officer. (Among those in his comically astute telephone circle: Richard Lewis, Carrie Fisher, and Rob Reiner.) Or he will watch television over the phone with many of these same friends, instructing them in which channel to tune in. He then supplies detailed commentary on what he sees, often while impersonating famous people. (His repertoire of mimicry is vast, ranging from Bob Hope to CNN anchor Bernard Shaw.) For example, as Rex Reed: "*Jessica Lllllange, marry someone else! You're getting bad advice!*" As George Bush (his excellent Bush, friends point out, predated Dana Carvey's version): "Wanna *preserve* the right of the hunter. At the same time, *don't* like to see those children shot. Maybe there's a compromise. Maybe we can send *deer* to school."

And when he can be no one else, he will resort to being a forty-three-year-old Jewish man who is always worried and who never laughs harder than when he is being laughed at. Or with. Or something.

Why He Lives Where He Lives

"As long as I've been supporting myself, I've always lived in the Valley. And I think about leaving all the time. But I look at it like this: I pretty much would be living the same life wherever I lived. I'm always afraid that if I get too far away from show business, I won't do it anymore. If I moved to a little cabin somewhere, I'm afraid I could sit and do nothing for too long. Here, at least, I can watch people zoom right by me."

You are there: the wrap party for *Defending Your Life*, May 1990, downtown Los Angeles. Mr. Brooks has taken over the large, swell club Vertigo for a full evening of celebration. Everywhere there is bounty: ice sculptures, grand buffets, free liquor, two bands, laughs aplenty. Mr. Brooks elects to arrive late, perhaps ninety minutes late, with his lovely female companion, the one called Cathy, a production coordinator on the movie. Now he is coming over here, propelled by his extraordinarily purposeful gait. His hangdog face betrays great discomfort. Now he speaks to you. "I look around this room," he says, finally, "and all I can do is wonder how this money could have improved my life."

From "Albert Brooks' Famous School for Comedians," a 1971 parody article he created for *Esquire*:

Q: Is life in comedy *always* fun?
A: No. But is anything *always* anything?

He is never on and he is never off. For this reason, he is considered less a comic, more an oracle. His name is spoken reverently by those who know comedy. To them he is Albert, simply Albert. As if to say, We are here, but he is Over There. His mind produces only pungent thought or, in essence, entertainment; there is no respite. Brain waves crash, pound, thunder, and permit him only three, maybe four hours sleep—usually while the TV flickers in the darkness. "It's disturbing," he says. "Of the last thirty dreams I've had, I've been on that show *Amazing Discoveries* in twenty of them. It must be because it's on at three in the morning. Or maybe I really do have a product to wash your car better than anyone else."

Of Mind and Man

"I don't think of him as being on in the same way that comics are on," says nonrelative Jim Brooks, comedy impresario (*The Simpsons, Broadcast News*). "I just think it *bursts* out of him. It's his way of communicating. It's *him*. His mind questions itself and never locks in. Listen, the big deal is never can you find a moment that wasn't a moment of absolute integrity. Never did he do something because the money was right. He's a comic *artist*, man. And he's one of the great comedy directors."

"Albert has always been one of the few people in my generation who has always been taken seriously in comedy," says *Saturday Night Live* godfather Lorne Michaels (the very fellow to whom Albert reportedly suggested the concept of different weekly guest hosts, having refused the full-time gig himself). "He plays to the top of the audience and he's paid a price for it, but not too great a price. It's very hard to get integrity late in life, and he's had it from the beginning." "He has a *huge* brain," says actress Kathryn Harrold, who was the object of Albert's affection in *Modern Romance* and, for a time thereafter, in life. "He's almost too smart for his own good."

Billy Crystal once told a *Playboy* interviewer the following story about a birthday party for Rob Reiner, boyhood chum of Albert Brooks's:

Albert Brooks had bought Rob some books. One was *Stunts and Games*. And Albert said, "Let me read you some of these things." Then he started making them up and reading them as if they were in the book: "This one's called National Football League. Get thirty of your friends together, have them donate five million dollars each to buy Black people who can run and hit." Or "Kennedy Assassination. Pretend you see smoke coming only from the Texas Book Depository, ignoring the man with the rifle in the tree standing next to you." I'd probably never seen anyone funnier in my whole life. In fact, it was so funny that he had to leave immediately afterward. I felt sad that Albert couldn't be a person; he had to leave.

Let us now ponder the Brooksian *oeuvre*, a small body of performances whose chief thematic link is desperation. Albert Brooks *is* the Desperate Man, a universally beset character crusading (mostly internally) for order and respect in a cold, capricious world. ("Wouldn't this be a great world," he asked, in *Broadcast News*, "if insecurity and desperation made us more attractive?") Pauline Kael, who once admiringly likened Albert's curled hair to brains worn outside of his head, has correctly observed, "When he's at his most desperate, he's funniest." As with many desperate lives, his personal desperation was honed as a stand-up comic. But it was immortalized in the seventies with a legendary *Tonight Show* appearance, wherein he announced that he had completely run out of material and proceeded to smash eggs into his hair, drop his pants, squirt himself with seltzer, rub pound cake on his face, and stalk offstage, bellowing the caveat, "This isn't the real me!"

Likewise, in his films, he dares to be pathologically, um, persistent. In *Real Life*, he fought to keep his documentary of an ordinary family from boring itself to death by asking the wife to have an on-camera affair with him. In *Modern Romance*, he ended his relationship with Kathryn Harrold in the first scene and fought for the rest of the film to reinstate it. ("Let me ask you something," his character, Robert Cole, says to Harrold's character, Mary Harvard, after waiting for her to return from a date with someone else. "If a person's not home, and you start driving around their house, and you drive around and around and around and around, and then you start driving around the city, and you're going ninety miles an hour, and you call 'em every four seconds, and you don't think about anything else, what is that? Is that not love?") In *Lost in America*, he was an adman who fought a lateral job transfer by dropping out of society to wander the country in a mobile home. Then, when his wife (played by Julie Hagerty) immediately lost their six-figure nest egg in a Las Vegas casino, he begged the pit boss to return their money as a public-relations gesture, suggesting as a campaign jingle: "*The Desert Inn has heart! The Desert Inn has heart!*"

"What distinguishes Albert's work," says Jim Brooks, explaining the Essential Albert Truth, "is that he totally sees how painful life can be. It's not like he's using humor as a cushion to make life more palatable. He's using his comedy to get further inside the pain."

Which brings us to *Defending Your Life*, whose title, even, is the apotheosis of desperation. In the opening moments, Albert drives into a bus and dies. He awakens in Judgment City, where he must wear strange linen gowns and account for his earthly lot by viewing tapes of terrible moments from his life (the perfect couch-potato fantasy!). If he proves that he faced up to his fears, he will "move forward" in the universe and become smarter. If not, he will be reincarnated on earth and try again. Meanwhile, he meets Meryl Streep and together they frolic and play miniature golf in the afterlife.

"Sure, it's optimistic," says Albert one afternoon in his Burbank office. "None of it takes place here." And as death goes, all in all, he'd rather be in Judgment City. "Nothing else ever made sense to me, and the only other thing I thought it might be was dirt, which I couldn't get financing for. Two hours of dirt—no one's gonna really put up much money. But my father died when I was eleven years old, which does start one out thinking, 'Gee, where did Dad go?' If nothing else, it forces you. I wasn't looking for answers as much as ideas. And so I started to look at what are the few things that bind us: What would make me the same as somebody who lives in Brazil or Haiti or Ethiopia or London? And basically, all human beings are frightened."

From *A Star Is Bought*, his classic 1976 comedy album: [*Reading tip: Albert plays both roles.*]

Psychiatrist: Do you still feel you can buy your friends with laughter?

Albert: [*Angrily*] Let me tell you something, *Doctor*. I don't have to buy my friends with anything. I don't *need* friends. I *shouldn't* have friends. . . . You don't go into this business and expect friends. I am a loner, I must be a loner—that's what an artist is!

Psychiatrist: You don't believe that.

Albert: [*Deflated*] You're damned right I don't believe that. Help me, man, I'm sick.

He was born a joke.

His father named him Albert Einstein, and his mother did not stop his father from doing so. His father was Harry Einstein, a radio dialect comedian known as Parkyakarkus (as in *park-a-your-carcass*) who worked with Eddie Cantor and Al Jolson. His mother is actress-singer Thelma Leeds. His older brothers were named Cliff (an adman) and Bob (a comic-actor, also known as deadpan-daredevil Super Dave Osborne). Albert, however, was called Albert, a human punch line with no choice but to live up to the name. (He switched to Brooks when he started performing, since, he says, "it sounded great with Albert. I tried Finney, but I got sued. I tried Prince, but it was taken. I tried Salmi and actually used it for two years.") They were the Einsteins of Beverly Hills adjacent, and showbiz was their life. "Everyone was fighting for ten minutes at the dinner table," says Albert, "with the youngest having the roughest time."

"I think Albert's father's absence is at least as large an event as anything in his present," says a friend, writer Paul Slansky. Indeed, Albert covets memories of his father, a wily, antic man, and shares them with zeal. We sat one morning in Art's Delicatessen, in Studio City, where he devoured matzo brie pancakes and regaled me with happy recollections. Like the time his family went to see the movie *Peyton Place*, and his father stood up at the end to sing loudly "Auld Lang Syne" with the cast. "I'm pulling him down, saying, 'Dad, please!'" Then there was the ritual of announcing to crowded restaurants that his youngest son was not eating his vegetables. "He would take his knife and for ten seconds just hit on the water glass"—alas, here Albert demonstrates—"until everyone was quiet. Then he'd say, '*Ladies and gentlemen, my little boy here . . .*' By then, I am not only eating the vegetables, I'm eating the farmer! I've gone back to the source. I'm eating all of *agriculture*."

His father died a great show-business death. He died onstage, at a Friar's Club roast, honoring Desi Arnaz and Lucille Ball. By this time, Harry Einstein was ill and semiretired but still an active Friar. "It was a dais of legendary performers," says Albert, "and my dad was on the dais and, the night before, I had helped him with his routine. He would talk very seriously and sincerely about the honorees and then miss their names: '*My closest friends in the world, Louise Bowls and Danny Arnaz!*' I never saw it, but he got up, and he was brilliant. It was elegant, and they screamed, and he sat down and passed on. Right there. They stopped the dinner and took him backstage—the classic '*Is there a doctor in the house!*' They cut him open backstage, shocked him with a lamp cord.

"The interesting thing," he says, hopefully, "is that he *finished*. That's what makes you believe in something. Whatever reason death comes, some-thing is here to make us finish. He didn't die in the middle of a line, and that's something."

The Impossible Truth! Did You Know That . . .

. . . Albert and Woody Allen once appeared on the same *Merv Griffin Show*! Afterward, Woody told Albert, "You're a funny man, Brooks." They have not spoken since, even though Albert has tried calling.

Once, there were no young comedians! Sensing this, Albert gave up plans to become a young actor and embarked upon a life of young comedy. "As an actor at nineteen," he says, "I was one of a thousand. As a comedian, I was one of two!" But first he completed three years at Carnegie Tech, in Pittsburgh.

His first comedy bit was that of the World's Worst Ventriloquist, whose dummy gurgled when Albert sipped water. Other early favorites: *Albért* the French mime, who described his every movement (*"Now I am walking up ze stairs"*); Alberto the animal trainer, whose elephant was lost, forcing him to make do with a frog; and the impressionist whose every offering sounded like Ed Sullivan.

Albert is an accomplished pianist, owns a clown suit, and holds ticket No. 70 on Pan Am's first flight to the moon, should one be scheduled. "Hell, I'm only glad it's not on Eastern," he says.

Albert will proudly tell anyone, "I am one of the longest wearers of contact lenses in the country!"

Often Albert's friends haven't known the last names of the women he dated— unless they were famous. Among these: Linda Ronstadt (they lived together), Candice Bergen, Julie Hagerty, and Harrold, who fondly remembers Albert's penchant for talking to livestock when driving through farmland. "If he saw a cow," she says, "he would always pull over and say, 'Hi, how are ya?'"

Albert *has* acted in other people's movies: You may remember him as the annoying campaign aide in *Taxi Driver*; as Goldie Hawn's dead husband in *Private Benjamin*; as the guy Dan Aykroyd eats in *Twilight Zone: The Movie*; and as conductor Dudley Moore's manager in *Unfaithfully Yours*. On *The Simpsons* he was the voice of Marge's amorous bowling instructor, Jacques.

Albert gave Michael Dukakis comedy lessons during his presidential campaign and wrote many jokes for the small governor. Dukakis, a reticent pupil, used only one. "I was trying to get him to be a little self-deprecating," says Albert. "The joke was, '*George Bush says it's time to give the country back to the little guy—here I am!*'"

"So I'm on trial for being afraid?" Albert says in *Defending Your Life*.

To overcome fear, he had to make a movie about overcoming fear. Fear has kept him hiding. Fear kept him from showing up in public as Albert Brooks, which kept America from remembering that there still is an Albert Brooks. His Carson appearances are now gauzy memory. Prior to this film, he had been a guest on the Letterman show exactly once. He last performed live in the days of the Druids. Woody, at least, makes a movie every year and is therefore difficult to forget. Steve Martin may never do stand-up again, but he sops media with aplomb. (Plus, unlike Albert, when Steve Martin is offstage, he is achingly sedate; a natural resource is not being wasted here.) Meanwhile, Albert's idea of exposure is to call Larry King in the dead of night and claim to be a Black decathlon athlete. People begin to talk.

"There are people throughout Hollywood who for a long time have theorized that Albert is afraid of success," says comedian Harry Shearer, who coproduced

A Star Is Bought and cowrote *Real Life*. "I don't think it's that simple. From a standpoint outside of his head, it's easy to say that Albert's too protective of himself. Because he's so good, you can bet that whatever it is that he's afraid of is clearly not going to happen. He's the comedian least likely to fail in a spontaneous situation, because he is so spontaneous. So it's sad that those explosively spontaneous gusts of comedy that Albert is more capable of coming up with than anybody aren't on public display. That side of him doesn't come through in his movies, where he's always extremely controlled. More than anybody else, he taught me the value of saying no in show business. But for my taste, he says it a little too often for his own good."

As cruel irony would have it, Albert once knew no fear. "I was abnormally fearless," he confesses, almost ashamedly. "I remember being offstage at *The Ed Sullivan Show*, talking to a friend on the telephone while I was being introduced! I wasn't even talking about the show—I was talking about *dinner*. My friend said, '*Hang up! You're on!*' I said *nonchalantly*: 'Oh. Okay.' I didn't even think about it. I wish I could have gone through my whole life that way. But unfortunately, it caught up with me. One day I said, '*Jesus!*' I was like the Road Runner. I ran a half-mile off the mountain, and then one day I looked down and went, 'Oh, my God!'

"Now, I don't think the object is to have *no* fear; it's to exist *with* fear. That seems healthy. To have no thought of fear isn't brave; it's a little crazy. Because when you finally do think of it, your equilibrium is thrown. The best combination is to say, '*This is scary and here I go.*'"

So, then, could he ever perform again?

"I think it might be great fun to do it again," he says, as though he possibly believes this. "Especially since life doesn't hinge on it. I'm a director now, so I don't have to be funny. One of the terrible things stand-up comedy can lead to, if you're not careful, is that your life starts to hinge on your performances. If it doesn't go well, your life stinks. I'd rather measure my life by my movies. Maybe I'd film it. Be interesting to see."

He stops and smells his own lack of conviction. "Edit this part out," he says, woeful and embarrassed. "That was all bullshit. It doesn't matter that I have another profession. It would still make me nervous. Because I'd still want it to be as good as it could be. And you couldn't convince me that it was all right not to be good, just because I had another job. You know? It's still the only game in town while you're doing it."

An epilogue: because there is nowhere else to put it, he keeps some comedy to himself.

Above the desk in Albert Brooks's office there hangs a framed letter. Few visitors ever notice it, but that is inconsequential. Badly typed on New York Yankees stationery, the letter is dated August 5, 1928, and is addressed to a Dr. Herbert Stevens, at Mount Sinai Hospital. It reads as follows:

Dear Dr. Stevens:
  Last Sunday when I visited Tommy on the fourth floor, I promised him I would hit a home run. As you may have heard, I grounded out four times that day. I understand that little Tommy has since passed on. In the future, I won't promise anything specific to the children. I'll just do what I can.

                                                                 My best,
                                                                 Babe

Albert's secretary typed the letter exactly as he had dictated it to her. She says that he has lately been asking her to find federal-prison stationery.

Albert Brooks: Albert Alone

Murray Murry / 1993

From *BUZZ*, November 1993, 62–64, 110. Reprinted with permission of Josef Vann.

When your father is a professional comedian named Harry Einstein who thought it would be really funny to name you Albert, you either learn to make people laugh yourself or you die. Albert Brooks, as he began calling himself shortly after he left college, chose the former. That didn't keep him from dying—numerous times, in numerous venues—but it did give him a career.

Today, after twenty-odd years (some of them very odd indeed) as a stand-up comic, actor, writer, and director (of such films as *Real Life, Modern Romance, Lost in America*, and *Defending Your Life*), Albert Brooks has earned himself a reputation as one of the funniest and most inventive comedians on the planet. "Albert was put on this earth to be a comic artist," says writer-director James L. Brooks, no relation but a longtime friend and colleague. "Whatever definition of art you come up with, it fits what Albert does."

What Albert has been doing most recently is acting (and singing and dancing) in Jim Brooks's soon-to-be-released musical movie *I'll Do Anything*, in which he costars as an incorrigibly insecure yet completely self-absorbed producer. You'd think a talent as wildly imaginative as Brooks would chafe at working under someone else's direction. Not necessarily. As Brooks told *BUZZ*'s Murray Murry in a recent conversation, there are times when not being in charge can be a positive blessing.

I love acting in other people's movies. Making my own films involves two years, twenty-four hours a day. If you act in someone else's movie, you're talking about six months, seventeen hours a day.

In *I'll Do Anything*, I got a very perverse enjoyment leaving the set at eight, watching Jim Brooks vomiting in the corner. I'd see him weeping in my rearview mirror. I really enjoyed the fact that it wasn't me.

The fact is, I consider myself lazy. I'm certainly not power-hungry. The only reason I started to direct was because I was writing. I mean, if I could write a

Real Life and hand it to someone else and know it would be made properly, I would do it. I'd much rather go to the beach.

I do what I do out of necessity, not out of ego. I remember an agent of mine was once frustrated with me. I had made a movie and the studio wanted some changes and I didn't know how to make them—I really didn't understand what they wanted—and the agent said to me, "I just don't understand why you always take the tougher road."

And I said, "You think I have a choice? You think there's an easy road and a tough road, and I say, 'See, I'm going to take the tough road?' Tell me where the easy road is—I'll back up."

I originally studied to be an actor. Even though I was naturally funny and could always make people laugh, I never once in my life said, "I want to do stand-up." My father, of course, was in radio, and I knew a lot of comedians. But when I first started, there weren't any comedy clubs. There was only Las Vegas. Comedians were old, they smoked cigars, and they worked in Nevada. That was the life of a comedian. What kid would want that? The cigar part, maybe.

So I never thought of it as a life for me. Instead, I studied acting at what used to be called Carnegie Tech in Pittsburgh; today it's Carnegie Mellon University. I was there for a couple of years, until a teacher I respected called me in one day and suggested I leave school. "Just go do it," he said. "School is a waste of your time."

So I came back to Los Angeles, and I tried to be an actor. But I couldn't get any parts. I was nineteen, and the only nineteen-year-old getting any roles back then was Richard Dreyfuss. I could, however, get work as a comedian, and the people in my life promised me that if I did that, the acting doors would open up.

So I started doing stand-up. I was opening for these hard-rock acts, which wasn't very much fun. For one thing, the audiences didn't know who I was. And depending on what drug they had taken, it could be real difficult quieting them down. You know, in the old days, when Bob Hope toured, he always had a couple of questions he'd ask before he went on in some strange town: "Who's the mayor? You got any rivers? What's the local car dealership?" My questions were: "What drugs have they taken? When did they drop? Do they wear shoes?"

But no acting doors opened up, just more and more comedian doors. Nobody was calling up and saying, "I want that funny guy in my movie." So there I was seven years later out on the road in Boston, waiting to do three shows, saying to myself, "Where the shit's the acting? What am I doing here?"

I mean, I like to be funny. But I don't feel the need to do it in front of a lot of people. That's my biggest problem, the thing that has probably frustrated all the agents and managers I've had: if I call you on the phone and I do schtick with you, that's as satisfying to me as if I did it on *The Ed Sullivan Show*. I mean that sincerely.

Some people need the world. Give me six people and I'm OK. That's why I've always had this problem in terms of doing comedy, especially where I had to do two and three shows a night. I never understood what the second and third shows were all about. I always wanted to come onstage and say, "Go find that first audience. They'll tell you it was funny. Good night!"

I made my first feature, *Real Life*, because of David Geffen. I had made a record album for Geffen, who then briefly became chairman of Warner Bros. While he was running the studio, he said to me, "Write a movie." And so I wrote *Real Life*. Then one day I passed him on the lot and he asked me, "How's it going?"

I said, "Fine."

He said, "*Hurry.*"

Shortly after that he left the studio, and in came a new regime that didn't know me from Adam. They thought I was parking cars.

"Who are you?" they asked me.

"I've written a script."

"Don't you work in the parking lot?"

So I didn't get *Real Life* made at Warner. But at least I had been funded to write it.

I then spent two years traveling across America trying to raise the money to make the movie. It was an experience I wouldn't wish on anybody. I met all kinds of people who said they had money and wanted to get into the movie business. In fact, all they wanted to do was get laid.

I remember meeting a guy in Dallas who owned a chain of dinner theaters. I pitched him my idea, and he said to me, "Al-buht"—he had this great drawl—"Al-buht, you know any hookers?" That's what he wanted. He wanted a hooker. I now work for him.

Actually, I finally found a guy in Chicago who was willing to put up half a million dollars for me to make *Real Life*. The guy didn't want to see the script or anything. He just wanted to be guaranteed that he would never have to put in a penny more than his original half a million. I was twenty-six at the time. I didn't own a house or anything, so the only way I could guarantee him that was to take all the money I had and get a loan from a bank that would provide me with another hundred thousand dollars if I needed it. Well, you can bet your life I didn't go over budget. This movie came in for four ninety-eight. I mean, I wasn't going to give up my car just so I could shoot another scene.

I joke about it, but it really is a lot of pressure. When the next dollar is yours, you don't fool around. Now, I know someone may read this and say, "Wow, that's the way movies should be made." In fact, it's not. There is so much pressure anyway on a movie set, you don't need to worry about your house being taken away.

To me, making a movie is like using one of those range-finder things they have on spaceships in science-fiction movies, where you're landing on the moon and the thing goes *beep-beep-beep* until you're lined up right in the center. That's what making a movie is. You just do it and do it and do it until you get the center. I don't mind beating myself to death making a movie. Because once you're through, you're through. You never have to think about it again. You can sit in the bath while it plays in Hungary.

Of course, when you're making movies you have to be willing to delay your gratification. You don't have that audience in front of you, responding. You just have to know that it's going to work. It's like a delayed orgasm. And this attitude has worked out well for me in sex, too. In fact, I think filmmakers are probably better lovers than stand-up comics. Although stand-ups are used to doing second and third shows.

I happened to be watching Stanley Kubrick's *2001* again the other day. Now, I don't care whether you like Kubrick's work or not, every frame of film that man has shot is brilliant. But I don't know what *2001* was about. I mean, people getting old after a light show and everything? And that monolith. What is it? Is it God? Twenty years ago, when the movie first came out, people stayed up all night arguing and arguing. And that's the way it should be.

Movies today don't give you enough of that. I'm not putting down any particular movie, but it's hard to see, say, *Rookie of the Year* and argue what it's about. "That twelve-year-old boy is God! I *know* he is!" We don't have those discussions.

I think it's nice when things are left a little bit what-does-it-mean? Because that's what art is for. I don't like to be hit on the head every day of my life: "This is what it means, this is what it means."

Unfortunately, that's precisely what's happened over the last few years in the movie business. People are so afraid that if the audience doesn't understand a hundred percent of a movie all the time, you've done something wrong. "Explain that, explain that," they tell you. "We're not so sure what it means. Explain it."

Who cares? Take it whatever way you want.

I never disagree with anybody who interprets anything I've done. I'm thrilled that people even bother.

You know, the seventies were just the greatest time for American films. Nobody ever talked about box-office grosses. People would talk about the *movie*. "And what did you think of the scene where he did that?" Now people who are in agriculture say, "I don't know, I don't think it's going to open."

There was a time in America, not too long ago, when nobody thought you were a fool if you went to a movie you wound up not liking. Then one day, it was like, "We want to protect you. We don't want you to waste your seven dollars."

What is that all about anyway? God forbid I should see two hours of something I'm not familiar with. Gee, I might learn something.

Reviewing movies became like a consumer report, like when you buy a Ford. And the only guideline was: Is it a hit? It was the same mentality as saying, "Go to McDonald's, they make the most popular cheeseburger in America."

Popular meant good. Well, I don't think that those two things are necessarily synonymous. Maybe sometimes. But, come on, there isn't time to make a list of all the brilliant people who ever lived who couldn't sell a thing. I don't think van Gogh cut off his ear because he was selling everything.

Anyway, they began to judge movies on whether people came or not. I was at the Sherman Oaks mall recently, and there was a line waiting to see some action movie. And I swear to God, this fat lady—who was definitely not in show business—actually said, "I heard this picture did *nine million* the first weekend."

That's what made her excited. It would be a nicer world if I had overheard her say, "I hear that the scene with the daughter is just devastating." But that's not what people are saying anymore. They used to. In college, you'd stay up all night arguing about movies.

"He was an asshole in that movie!"

"What are you, crazy? He was *wonderful.*"

Not anymore. God knows what they're talking about in college now.

"That movie won't stay in the theaters two weeks!"

I still have hope that these four million cable channels we're going to get will help change things. The best thing that can ever happen to the arts in my opinion is narrow casting. Getting three million people to leave their homes and go see a movie doesn't make anyone very much money. But if you can get three million people to press a button one night to watch something on their cable system, everyone's going to do very well.

So narrow casting gives us the potential to appeal to a smaller audience and still be able to please the businessmen. It will be very good for experimentation.

Of course, there is a difference between watching a movie at home and watching one in a theater. The thing about the movies that has always been the most fun is the strangers: sitting for two hours with people you don't know in a place that is not your own, reacting.

You don't often sit with strangers and have emotional experiences. That's what the theaters offer. Unfortunately, everything that is happening now in terms of the technology, from QVC to home shopping to Home Box Office, is working to eliminate that experience. The only positive aspect of that is that it may allow more people to experiment without the money people feeling that they are going to lose their shirts.

But what will never be duplicated is the experience of walking into a building that has nothing to do with you. It's an event; it gives us a chance, without having to say anything, to check off with each other. It's like smelling the behind of another monkey. "Look, we're all laughing; look, we're all crying." If you don't come out of your house, you lose all that. And that would be bad, because I believe that the shared experience with strangers is wonderful.

When I'm working alone, I do my writing on a tape recorder. That's because I can talk much faster than I can type. Also, with a tape recorder I can do a lot of voices and play the different characters. In addition, my tape recorder can go anywhere. So sometimes I get in my car and drive. Because of its movement, the automobile forces you to keep thinking. You know, you're driving, the trees are going by—it's like a rhythm.

But I can work anywhere. It may sound corny, but if the muse is willing to come sit with you, you can write in the hospital. It doesn't matter where you are. You just get the idea or you don't.

Most of my ideas seem to be things I've already thought of. They seem to be in there, and all I'm doing is rearranging them. It's like a Chinese menu: taking one from column A and one from column B. That's why, to me, writing is like solving this *big puzzle*.

I remember reading a book called *The Soul of a New Machine* by Tracy Kidder. In it, he described a guy who designed computer chips, and he sounded exactly like me. I remember he was going to a barbeque one Sunday and every street looked to him like a path electricity would take on a circuit board. Well, that's just it. When you get in the middle of writing a script, people are talking to you and you're nodding, but you're like on Mars, you know.

For me, writing and making movies is scary. That's because any movie I make changes me. Either I meet a person or I learn something about myself. But I've never been the same at the end of a movie as I was going in.

The thing is, you can never figure out in advance how the experience is going to change you. In fact, the more you anticipate, the more wrong you'll be. Life doesn't like it when you anticipate. I think if there is a God, he's not crazy about you figuring it out. "Gee, I'll have to show little Stevie that maybe he's not so smart. Here, *multiple sclerosis!* Now raise your hand, you moron!" I don't like to fool around with that.

It's Albert

Alison Rose / 1994

From the *New Yorker*, February 14, 1994, 40–47. Reprinted with permission.

Albert Brooks was at home, he said, sitting on the edge of his bed. I was sitting on my bed at the Regent Beverly Wilshire. It was my last morning in Los Angeles. Monica Johnson, who wrote the movies *Real Life, Modern Romance*, and *Lost in America* with Brooks, had said to *make* him take me "for a spin" in his white Miata. She said, "It's very fast. Wear a scarf." Albert yelled at me now when I suggested the spin. Albert yelled, "NO MORE SPINS!" There isn't type big enough to show how loud and hardhearted he sounded. Then he said, "I could thrill you so much. I'm tempted to do this for you," and he said he would play me the tape of the last evening of his father's life, when his father died—literally—in front of twelve hundred people at the Friars Club. First, Albert went rummaging around trying to find the tape. He said he hadn't listened to it in years. I could hear him shuffling tapes, dropping them, and humming in a jittery, loud way. He came back on the phone. "I'll go in the other room and sit down at a phone that's more comfortable for me and see if you can hear it," he said. There was a silence. Then he played the tape.

It was a tape of a testimonial dinner for Lucille Ball and Desi Arnaz in November of 1958 at the Beverly Hilton. I heard Art Linkletter reading a telegram to Lucy and Desi from Eddie Cantor. Then Linkletter introduced Albert's father: "A great guy and a fine Friar, Harry Einstein—Parkyakarkus." (In movies and on radio, Albert's father played Eddie Cantor's Greek sidekick; the name is pronounced "Park Your Carcass.") Then Brooks's father was telling a lot of jokes, in what Brooks called his Winston Churchill voice, about "my very dear and close friends Miss Louise Bowl and Danny Arnaz." The audience was so carried away that finally all I could hear except hilarity was silverware crashing and the Desi Arnaz maniacal Cuban laugh. Brooks got back on the phone, convulsed, and managed to say, "Do you hear Desi laughing?" He turned off the tape and said, "So he walks back to the dais . . . and he puts his head on the table. That's it."

It is quite possible to live in America and not know about Albert Brooks, especially if you didn't see *Broadcast News*, in which he plays Holly Hunter's unglamorous suitor—the one who moans, "Wouldn't this be a great world if insecurity and desperation made us more attractive?" He has acted in movies by such directors as Martin Scorsese (*Taxi Driver*) and James L. Brooks (*Broadcast News* and the newly released *I'll Do Anything*), and has written, directed, and acted in four of his own movies: *Real Life*, in 1979; *Modern Romance*, in 1981; *Lost in America*, in 1985; and *Defending Your Life*, in 1991. But none of his own movies were successful in the strictest, commercial sense, and in certain Hollywood circles Brooks is regarded as someone with an unerring instinct for offbeat, unmarketable projects. It would be stretching things to talk about an Albert Brooks "cult," but nevertheless there is a sizable population of Albert Brooks fanatics, who watch his movies over and over again and can quote his early stand-up routines from memory.

Among his peers, Brooks is an object of veneration that has nothing to do with box office. Famously funny people speak about him with awe. Steve Martin, who first became an admirer twenty-five years ago, calls Albert Brooks the Richard Feynman of the comedy world and adds, "He is someone you respect and fear at the same time, because of his brilliance. Fear in the sense you just *know* something's going on there all the time." Charles Grodin worked for Brooks ("for nothing," he says, meaning for scale) in Brooks's first movie, and even read for his part (as established actors generally do not), because, he says, "I wanted to serve him." The director Garry Marshall told me that once, a few years ago, when he was a guest on *Late Night with David Letterman*, Letterman had talked to him about Brooks all during a commercial break. "He's above all of us. I mean, he's up there and we're down here when it comes to the real humor, Letterman said." Marshall added, "Some of the public doesn't know it, but we who do this for a living know." Many of those people echo Johnny Carson, who said of Brooks, "I can't wait to see what he does next."

Carl Reiner told me—in startling detail—about a routine Brooks had done thirty years ago, at age sixteen, in the Reiner living room. The routine sounded like the kind of vaudeville inversion that brought Albert Brooks, at twenty-eight, to the notice of *Saturday Night Live*. In the routine Reiner remembers, Brooks was an escape artist trying to wiggle loose from a handkerchief laid over his wrists. "Prodigy comedy people are rare," Reiner went on. "You have to be a little older to make people laugh, but here I said, 'Well, *there's* a mind at work.' It made me laugh so hard I couldn't breathe."

By way of explaining Albert Brooks's relative lack of fame, Mel Brooks said once on *Larry King Live*, "I think he doesn't want the responsibility of being a star. Because he could have it. . . . He just simply doesn't *want* to be famous."

Pauline Kael may have been closer to the mark when she wrote appreciatively of Brooks, "Everything he does is odd." Or, as the director Michael Ritchie put it, "People don't think any human mind works that way." In every character that Albert Brooks has created, including his stand-up personae, he takes a kind of extreme longing and makes it comedic, and in the process seems to imply—either arrogantly or hilariously, depending on whom you ask—that his worldview is the only acceptable one.

I've noticed, by the way, that nearly all the people who insistently call Brooks "funny" ("He's funny! He's just *funny!*") are men. He makes women laugh out loud as well, but "funniness" is not what they mention first. They are more likely to speak of his effect on them—to say that their laughter feels like a complete loss of control but a loss without danger. They say things like "It's better than sex," and, when they amplify, it becomes clear that for them his greatest talent is for saying or conveying things that they had never had the nerve to come out with, even to themselves.

Men and women agree that Albert Brooks's comedy is predicated on a short fuse. He's inordinately impatient with the little hoops of "everyday life." The impatience expresses itself not merely as irony; his humor is an overturning. Any number of comics make fun of neurosis; Brooks takes it as a given—as the fabric of American life—and in his movies and elsewhere it is "well-adjustedness" that seems outré or repellent, or simply off.

Albert Brooks is six feet tall, and strong-looking. He has curly brown hair and distracted greenish-brown eyes. His voice, the way he talks, his inflections become contagious if you spend any time in his company. If I'm in a Korean grocery store nowadays, I might say to myself, "*All* right. Let's get the *blue*berries." That's the way Brooks would say it, as if any other possibility were an irremediable mistake. Sometimes, as he speeds along, talking, he'll reverse himself abruptly. Often, he can sound like a bully, or a lecturing schoolteacher. There's a scene in *Lost in America* in which the wife (Julie Hagerty), having lost the family savings gambling in Las Vegas, refers to their "nest egg," and he says to her, "Please do me a favor. Don't use the word. *You may not use that word.* It's off limits to you. Only those in this house who *understand* 'nest egg' may use it. And don't use any *part* of it, either. Don't use 'nest.' Don't use 'egg.' If you're out in the forest, you can *point.*"

Albert's voice never dives down low, and it never quite rises to a shriek, either. It's within the range of a normal man's voice, but it often sounds agitated. He can also be extremely persuasive. David Geffen, who has been Albert's financier over the past twenty years and whose company produced *Lost in America* and *Defending Your Life*, said, "When we're about to engage in making a movie, sometimes you'll hear from him eight times a day. Or a *hundred* times a day, if he wants something very badly that you're not willing to give him. He'll call you all night and all day."

Brooks's accent doesn't sound like Boston, where his father was from, or New York, where his mother grew up, but it doesn't have the usual flat Southern California tone, either, although he was born in Los Angeles and has lived there almost all his life. Sometimes a weird twang enters his speech; on an answering machine he might say, "It's AEELbert." Sometimes he does other people's voices. Johnny Carson told me about Albert's Burt Lancaster voice, which he once produced on the air by putting a hot potato in his mouth. (When I asked Brooks about this, he said, "I threw this hot potato in my mouth, and just to cool it down I went, 'Hhhah . . . Hhhah'—you know, like the beginning of what Burt Lancaster sounds like.") Carson laughed so hard he had to get out of his chair and grab hold of the backdrop curtain. NBC used a clip of Johnny, hands to his eyes, laughing at Albert's Burt Lancaster voice for years in promotions for the show.

Brooks has one laugh that sounds as if it were coming from the bottom of a coal mine. He laughed this laugh into a microphone about ten times in a row one morning while he was taping a movie loop in a fairly dark room at Sony Pictures, and some of us watching began keeling over with silent, forbidden laughter. The loop was for *I'll Do Anything*. Up on the screen, Albert, a movie producer, was in the back seat of a car, with Nick Nolte in the driver's seat. Albert added a raucous cough to the laugh and roared into the microphone. He didn't sound anything like Albert Brooks. Most of the time, Albert's laugh is like an invitation to a secret club, and people seem to want to glue themselves to it for as long as they can. Carrie Fisher told me of how, at a certain point in her life, she and Albert would drive to Palm Springs, a two-hour ride: "Nonstop talking the entire way. *Screaming* and joking and yelling. And then we'd drive straight back, so we did it for four hours. We never got out of the car. We would just wreck each other." At moments like that, when he's spinning through one of his marathon monologues—when he's nearly incandescent—Albert sometimes doesn't laugh at all.

Albert Lawrence Einstein was born on July 22, 1947. (He changed his last name to Brooks in 1967, because "Albert Einstein," he told me, was never a tenable stage name.) His father had moved from Boston to Los Angeles around 1930 and met Thelma Leeds, who was a singer and actress, when they were both contract players on the RKO lot. They were married by the time they were appearing in the revue *New Faces of 1937*. Albert has three older brothers: the oldest, Charles Einstein, is Harry's son by a first marriage and is a well-known sportswriter; the second, Clifford Einstein, is an advertising man; and Bob Einstein is the comedian Super Dave Osborne (he also played the sporting-goods salesman in *Modern Romance*).

When Harry Einstein was still alive, the family lived in a house on Benedict Canyon Drive, just outside Beverly Hills. "It was a regular house, right next to other houses," Brooks said when I asked him about it. "It had a pool. It had green grass and a yard. There weren't any sidewalks." Inside the house, "you sort of had to be quiet," Albert told me, because of his father's heart condition, and added that he was "off into my head for the most part, making up stuff in my room." Every day, he thought, *this* is the day my father's going to die. Harry Einstein's radio career ended when Albert was a year old, so Albert was able to hear his show, *Meet Me at Parky's*, only on records. "I listened to them alone in my room," he told me, and he went on to say, "When my dad died, my older brother Cliff—he sounds like me—became sort of the dad, and my mother and I fought. Then my mother married a lovely man that I was crazy about, and they stayed married for twenty-some years, until he died. He was in the shoe business—ladies' shoes." Albert put a little spin on "ladies' shoes" but then said, "He was on my side immediately. I was the smallest and the youngest. And he was very handsome but sort of short. So we just had a lot in common."

One evening before I went out to California but after I'd spoken to Brooks on the phone, I rented all his movies. I put the 1979 *Real Life* in the VCR and there was Albert in a cowboy shirt, with a pale-pink scarf around his neck. *Real Life* is a mock documentary—a director's psychosociological, "scientific" footage of an all-American family. The film crew's hidden cameras look like washing machines that fit over their heads. About thirty-five minutes into the film, the pure science begins to crumble. Frances Lee McCain—she plays Jeanette Yeager, the all-American wife—asks Brooks (the documentary's director) to meet her in private. They're standing in front of a shop window, and though Albert seems to put his arm around her, he keeps about two and a half inches of space between his arm and her back. When he pats her to comfort her, he's patting the air. After this deformed embrace, Mrs. Yeager says, "You're such a sensitive man" and "You gave me the strength," and kisses him. When she walks to her car, he spits the kiss out, wipes his mouth, and shouts after her, "I gave you nothing, Mrs. Yeager! No, no . . . I gave you *nothing!* Really. Don't think I'm anything better than what you have. You think I've got this charisma, but I don't! I really don't. . . . Oh, I have a *little* bit of it. But it just sits on the surface. It doesn't run deep. Now, no kissing here." He's still yelling after her: "I'm a shallow fellow. Look!" He's holding out his left forearm, the palm of his right hand going back and forth about three inches above it. "SHALLOW, SHALLOW! Really. *Shal-*

low!" The movie ends with Albert in a clown suit, a torch in his hand, burning down the all-American family's house.

I watched Brooks in three movies that night, and when I was trying to fall asleep I thought about the scene in *Broadcast News* when his character, a network news reporter, has to go on as the anchor without much warning and Holly Hunter, who plays his producer, looks at him, takes the shoulder pads out of her evening gown, and puts them in the shoulders of the jacket he's wearing. He lets her do it. Here was the underside of Albert's onscreen persona. The short fuse doesn't go off—it goes dead. He can express resignation more poignantly than almost anyone else.

There are Brooks fans who think the essence of his work was embodied in the short films he did for *Saturday Night Live* in its first season, 1975–76. In one of them, Brooks plays a filmmaker talking about his films. A little blond girl, playing his attention-starved daughter, comes up and bites him on the hand. He has a policeman take her away. "You won't be seeing her again," he says blandly in a voice-over. Then he shows a home movie about himself—the filmmaker as a boy. His father has a movie camera and follows him around: Albert going to the bathroom for the first time by himself, Albert kissing his first girl. Finally, the father comes barging into a room where Albert is making love for the first time. "He's nice," the voice-over comments about the father. "I see him about twice a year now."

Lorne Michaels says, "I had a sort of blind admiration for Albert. We worked together about twenty-five years ago. He was doing the Danny and Dave routine then. And, of course, I had seen *Albert Brooks' Famous School for Comedians"*—a fake commercial with a beaming Albert giving us a tour of the "institution"—"and I'd seen him on *The Tonight Show* lots of times. In 1975, when I got to do *Saturday Night*, I wanted him to be a performer. Failing that, I asked him, would he host it occasionally, and failing *that*, would he make short films. It was all he wanted to do, and I wanted him desperately. He was everything I wanted the show to be in terms of its comedic voice. I think all that ever mattered to Albert—at least, in the period that I knew him well—was the work. There were contending wills, but he was very gentle with me."

Talking to me once about Danny and Dave, an act he invented when he was barely twenty, Brooks sounded as excited as if he'd just thought it up. "Dave was the world's worst ventriloquist," he said. "He never tried to hide his mouth moving, and I had this stupid voice for the dummy." Later on, when I watched a tape of Danny and Dave from an *Ed Sullivan Show*, I saw a very young, puppyish Albert throwing the dummy Danny on the floor, face down, to get his hands free so he can light a cigarette. When he gives Danny a glass of water while Dave sings, he pours the water all over Danny's face, and the water runs down onto the floor. Johnny Carson told me, "Danny and Dave—it just put me away."

In 1976, Brooks and Lorne Michaels had a falling out—over Albert's feeling that his contributions to *Saturday Night Live* had been slighted, one gathers—and they have had little contact since. David Geffen says, "You know, it's hard to hang in there with Albert . . . but I'm a believer. And I don't give up easily." Like the characters Brooks has written for himself, he can think and talk from more angles than most people, and his friends sometimes find him unrestrained. The writer and director Harvey Miller, who has known Brooks for years, said in an abrupt moment, gruffly, "Too many phone calls. Too much coming over." At other times, Brooks just disappears—"goes underground," as he calls it—with little explanation. It's as if things have to be on his terms or not be at all.

When Brooks directs a movie—or acts in one, for that matter—he doesn't behave that way. Of Brooks as an actor, Holly Hunter has said, "He reveals himself, shockingly so. . . . He's ridiculously truthful." As a director, he seems to use his insight into his fears as a way of showing empathy with his actors. Hunter says, "He illuminates your scariest thought without distracting himself from people."

Julie Hagerty told me, "He just *makes* things come true." She was speaking of Brooks as an actor, in the nest-egg scene, but it's also true of him as a director: he startles his colleagues with this ability, perhaps after first puzzling them. Meryl Streep said she'd hurt his feelings once when, after many excited invitations, he took her out to Orange County to show her the location of the Past Lives Pavilion in *Defending Your Life*. He'd found the perfect place, he told her, and when she remarked that it looked "like an industrial park in New Jersey," he seemed crushed. In his mind, he was seeing something else altogether. When she saw the film, she was startled to discover that he'd been exactly right.

While Brooks's friends are frank about how exasperating he can be, the devotion with which they talk about him is remarkable. They recount phone calls with him in a way that reminds you of the RCA Victor dog listening with rapt attention to His Master's Voice. They tell affectionate stories about his new house, which he moved into last year, or his old ones. And they recount the smallest, everyday encounter with him as if they'd just come blinking out of a movie theatre where it was featured. The production designer, screenwriter, and producer Polly Platt once told me, "You know the other house—the one he moved out of? No one was allowed there. Somebody would deliver a package to his house and they'd have to leave it at the gate, and he would wait, like Buster Keaton. Then he would go out and snatch the package and bring it in."

His women friends talk about him in a semihovering fashion. "I always wonder what he does, you know, with his life," Polly Platt said to me on another occasion. "What does Albert *do*? Sometimes I think he spends a lot of solitary time practicing some of his stories and jokes. If you ever see anyone who does magic tricks very well, you realize it means a lot of lonely, solitary practicing. I think he requires that seclusion."

Penny Marshall, who was once married to Rob Reiner (who grew up with Albert and went to Beverly Hills High School with him), told me about the gatherings at their house in the seventies. "Jim Brooks, Harvey Miller, Jerry Belson, Chuck Grodin, Louise Lasser, Richard Dreyfuss—Albert was always the funniest," she said. "Then he had a slight nervous-breakdownish thing, when he was touring to promote his comedy album. He came over to our house and sort of stayed there on the couch, but it was the funniest breakdown you've ever seen."

Albert's sometime cowriter Monica Johnson says, "Sometime in the mid-seventies, I'd heard *Comedy Minus One*"—Albert's first album—"at Rob and Penny's house and was dying to meet him. Penny brought him to my house, in Dixie Canyon. He had his big curly hair and his twinkling eyes, and he went straight to the M&M's. It was like someone had brought over this brand-new toy. Oh my God! Anything in the room was a prop. He could sustain it for an hour, to an audience of one. It was like having a radio show come to your house. Later, we'd drive around looking for the best chicken—the ride was the thing. We would drive up the coast, to the desert, through the canyons. We did some of the movie writing in the car. For a short time while we were writing *Modern Romance*, Albert had a silver Cadillac Seville. I remember we were stalled behind this big truck—this was on Ventura Boulevard, near Sepulveda—and we were sitting there talking and talking, and suddenly we realized there was no one at the wheel of the truck. It had just parked there."

Brooks doesn't like his friends to talk about where he lives, but Monica broke the rules and said, "There was that house he rented on Pacific View Drive, off Mulholland. Just a little house, a very bachelor existence. And half-hanging on a hanger in a closet was the clown suit he wore in *Real Life*. He also had a camera setup. The whole house was like a great playground studio. Anyway, then he moved to a house on Yoakum Drive in Benedict Canyon, kind of small. I remember he always had a lot of stuff stored in his garage. Things I had never seen before—like a big diagram of how a joke works. He had gone to the trouble to diagram it. And Danny was in there, sitting in a box. He was just a typical dummy. Straight black hair."

When I was getting dressed to meet Brooks for the first time, he called me from his car to say it was *hot*, he didn't *feel* well, and could he pick me up in half an hour? I had to turn off the radio, and when I got back on the phone I told him I hadn't put on mascara yet. "OK," he said, in his most bullying voice. "You've got twenty-two minutes per eye." And then, as if he recognized stage fright, he also said, "You already *know* me."

When I went down to the hotel lobby, I saw him sitting in a fake-French chair in front of a heavy pink curtain. He was dressed all in black: short-sleeved silk shirt, trousers, sneakers, sunglasses with black rims. He was chewing gum. When he saw me and stood up, he seemed taller than he does on screen. He looked like a tough man who was in a bad mood.

The car he was driving was a blue-gray Mercedes 300 E, and on our way out of Beverly Hills he drove with only one hand. I made an effort not to think about the way he got killed in *Defending Your Life* (his BMW hits a bus). The outdoor-temperature indicator on the dashboard said ninety-six degrees. The windows were shut and the air conditioner was on. We went to Santa Monica and then on to Malibu. He told me the background of his career in a matter-of-fact tone: after his appearances on national TV in the late sixties, he'd started doing stand-up live, in clubs and college auditoriums. But in 1974, he said, he stopped performing for a year. Stand-up wasn't getting him movies—it was just getting him more stand-up. "I wasn't old enough to make an intelligent decision, so I sort of sent myself into a tailspin," he said. "Then I *couldn't* do it, so I rested for a year." In 1975 came the *Saturday Night Live* films. They led to acting in other people's movies (the first one was *Taxi Driver*, in 1976, in which he played a zealous presidential-campaign worker), and then writing and directing his own full-length films and acting in them.

I had been hearing endlessly about Albert's new house, but he hadn't said a word about it. James Brooks told me, "You should know Albert's new house is a major, major—it was a big deal for him to get himself a house like that. Words fail me." His friend David Kipper said, "Have you been to the Ahwahnee Hotel, in Yosemite? Albert's house is going to remind you of the Ahwahnee."

Sitting in the car, I said, "David Kipper told me you have an eagle's nest in your back yard."

"Yes," Albert said, in an ambiguous voice. "I have three eagles in a tree near me. I went to a bookstore and looked them up, and they seem to be golden eagles. They started out cute, but they're bigger now than I am, and they make more noise than a dog. They make this whistle. It's an unflattering bird sound. But they're amazing to watch. I bought binoculars, and I watched them learn how to fly. First of all, their nest is bigger than my room. It's eight feet long, I swear to God. You and I could get in there and get a good night's sleep. They go from the nest to an upper branch and back, over and over and over. Then to a little higher branch, and back. That's what they do. They hop back and forth in the same tree for about a week. Then, eventually, they move to a nearby tree. Then they fly freely, and now I'm waiting for them to leave."

"Because of the whistling?"

"Yes. I've given them hints. I've put brochures of Alaska all over the tree."

"How did you first notice them?"

"I noticed the mother finishing up the nest. And sitting there and taking care of something."

"How did you know it was a mother?"

"Well, I don't know. Do *men* sit on eggs? I didn't see a vagina, if that's what you mean, but I just assumed the mother sits on eggs."

At some point on our way back to Beverly Hills, I asked if he would show me his house. He said no, in several ways, and then explained: "All I do for a living is be exposed. That's all I am. I'm *exposed*. So if I didn't have the one little area that's not exposed, a few inches, I'd go nuts. I can tolerate if a person thinks I'm fat or thin or ugly. I can read that in the newspapers and be OK. . . . But once, a long time ago, I let somebody come into a house, and they wrote about—they didn't like—the room looked *dark* to them. *That* bothered me. Because I live there. My house isn't onstage, *I* am." After a pause, he went on, "I guess it would hurt me more to read about my taste than to read about my talent, because I can say 'You're crazy if you don't like my talent,' but if you put my taste down I might doubt it." His voice changed. "I'm not that secure."

When Brooks leaves a phone message, he's likely to begin, "It's *A*lbert," and then, "Are you there?" When I got back from California, we began speaking on the phone, sometimes at length. He seemed happier talking to a journalist long-distance instead of in person. I noticed that at the end of a call, almost as a substitute for "goodbye," he would say, "You call me if you need me." He never sounds as if he were doing something else over the phone besides talking. He's not putting on his shoes or doing the dishes. Sometimes he would call from his car (if the connection got broken in the tunnel, he'd call right back, in case I thought he'd hung up) or from home in the afternoon, but usually he'd call from home on Saturdays at around 9:20 a.m. New York time, 6:20 a.m. in California.

There is no satisfactory way to shorten one of Brooks's marathon telephone monologues for the page. In any given hour-plus call there would be several long loops of thought, and shorter speech rhythms within them; punctuating jokes, like little melodies; disconcerting silences. His voice and his mood would sink and rise, and he would leap and swoop from one thing to another, and tear into thought patterns so complicated you never knew how he was going to tie them together, or even sort them out, but he never failed. Without a single flaw in logic, he could go from talking about his ticket for Pan Am's first moon flight to the naïveté of early telephone operators to a weatherman in Des Moines. Periodically during these conversations, he would wind down and then would swerve in some unfathomable direction and be off again, swinging from affection to scorching harshness but staying on the phone.

Albert often has a hard time getting off the phone. One Saturday morning, we'd been talking for an hour and a half—about everything from apple fritters to "why the Bible could never be true." Since I wasn't allowed to see his new house, I'd begun asking to *hear* things in his house. He'd played me his keyboard (organ, piano, string samples, then rhythm: "Here's Boogie . . . Here's Beguine . . . Mambo . . . Samba") and he'd played me his piano ("Cocktail music: nobody drives here to hear it"), and now he said, "I bought a good fan yesterday. Do you ever buy fans?"

I told him I had, a year ago.

"Well, there's a thing called a Vornado. It's small, but, boy, is it *powerful.*"

"What's it called?"

"VORNADO," he said loudly.

"With a 'V'?"

"Yeah," he said in a half whisper.

"Like a 'tornado,' only with a 'V'?"

"That's right. Exactly. They got some gimmick. I mean, it's like small, but it's wonderful. Geez, 'It's wonderful'—look what we're talking about. I'm going to *kill myself.* We're talking about a fan!"

I wondered why that was depressing, but then he asked, "What did *you* buy?"

I said I'd got an oscillating one and wasn't crazy about it.

"*Yeah.* It's like a bus going by. I keep getting up and looking for something. It comes with *announcements* 'NOW ARRIVING, FLIGHT 44.' I *hate* that. No, this doesn't oscillate. No, this stays in one place and blows the air seventy, seventy-five feet without the air moving away from the column. It's not a big deal, but it's very quiet. Want to hear it over the phone? Here's at top speed." There was the sound of Albert playing his Vornado into the phone. It sounded like a flock of birds—maybe doves—all shoved together and in a big hurry. "That's the thing right there."

When I asked him what that sounded like to him, he got into a fifteen-minute story about the wind at the North Pole, and a three-minute story about the Red Sea waters, and then, after a silence, he said, "Well, OK. I guess I'll get up. I'll take a little walk, have some coffee, and get my day going." He paused. "OK." He said OK on three notes, almost parrot-voiced. I could tell we were close to hanging up. Then he was saying, "You call me if you need me. Goodbye."

Problem Child

David Handelman / 1997

From *Premiere*, January 1997, 76–80, 92. Reprinted with permission.

Albert Brooks was elated—well, about as elated as a comedian can get, anyway. Paramount had just greenlighted *Mother*, his new effort as cowriter-director-star, about a grown man who blames his midlife crisis on his hypercritical, withholding mother, and decides to move back in with her, hoping to resolve their relationship. Brooks felt that *Mother* could be a real breakthrough, personally and maybe even commercially, and he did what any excited, loyal son would do: he called his own mother, now in her eighties, to tell her the good news.

"Honey, that's wonderful," she replied. "But the acting jobs just aren't coming, huh?"

Brooks tells this story with a wry smile. "I thought, 'Oh boy, I can't *wait* to make this! Am I right on! I gotta make this, quick!'"

The urge was uncharacteristic: when it comes to moviemaking, Brooks is not known for speed. "Albert works at his own pace," says David Geffen, whose former company funded two Brooks films. What kind of pace is that? "*Very* slowly."

Brooks himself admits, "I'm like the third little pig—I just plod along." He spent nearly twelve years figuring out the screenplay for this last auteur-actor-effort, *Defending Your Life*—which came out in 1991.

The irony is that Brooks is one of the quickest wits on the planet—a comedian's comedian. He's not "on" in the annoying way; he simply can't help seeing life's absurdities and producing entertaining lines in a nanosecond. (After all, his given name was Albert Einstein.) Even the act of ordering health-conscious lunch at the Paramount commissary becomes grist for a routine. "I'd like a turkey burger," he tells the waiter. "I don't see the heart next to it—does that mean it's bad? Does the chef spit on it? Why does the chicken burger have one? Could we move the heart over?"

"When Albert goes four years between movies," says his manager Herb Nanas, "I'm the only one who has the pleasure of laughing every day, because we speak on the phone. And after I hang up, there's always that moment of despair: why doesn't the world hear this?"

Last summer, if you happened to be among the few who caught a little movie called *Mission: Impossible*, you would have witnessed a coming attraction that ranks among the most self-deprecating in Hollywood history. Devised by Brooks's ad exec big brother, Cliff, it begins with a close-up of a cellular phone being dialed; for a moment, you think maybe it's *Mission: Impossible*. Then you see Brooks talking into the phone, sitting in a director's chair on a movie set: "Hello, Mother. . . . Finished my new movie, and I'm very excited—no, I didn't retire. . . . You know who plays my mother? The legendary Debbie Reynolds! No, she's not dead. . . . Anyway, Paramount Pictures is really happy with it. Paramount. Yes, the real one! Yes, the one with the mountain. . . . Yes, I hope it does better than the last one too. Oh no, Mother, don't worry, it's not about you. Love you!" Then a techie asks Brooks for the chair, and when he stands up, you see that it's inscribed "TOM CRUISE."

Funny, yes. But will it sell tickets? "I never really liked that piece that much," says *Mother* producer Scott Rudin, otherwise a huge Brooks fan. "And I frankly urged Albert not to do it, because I thought it was preaching to the converted." It's true. If you had never seen or liked Brooks, you probably would have wondered, Is this guy pathetic? He made a movie about his mother? He doesn't own a chair? Where's Tom Cruise?

Seeking mass acceptance for the precise, squirmy, giddy movies of Albert Brooks can seem as futile as whispering during a screening of *Twister*. *Defending Your Life* boasted his biggest budget (sixteen million dollars), biggest costar (Meryl Streep), and biggest high-concept premise (what is death like?), but didn't break Brooks out of his cult. He's in that select pop-culture elite—like Elvis Costello, say, or *The Larry Sanders Show*—where artist and audience see eye-to-eye but the rest of the world always seems to be off reading *The Bridges of Madison County*.

When Paramount saw his *Mother* trailer, Brooks says, "the studio thought, 'Okay that'll play well enough in the big cities, but will it play in Kansas City?' I've been dealing with that question my entire life. The first day I was ever in show business, the producer of *The Dean Martin Show* looked at my routine and said, 'I know they'll get it here, but what about . . . ?' He used Des Moines. So in twenty-seven years, I've come two hundred miles. My opinion is, I don't think Kansas City is any different anymore, or *Seinfeld* wouldn't be the number one show. And the malls all wouldn't look alike."

Seinfeld or no, Brooks is still a misfit at the multiplex. He's been called the West Coast Woody Allen—enough so that he turned down the lead in *When*

Harry Met Sally . . . because, he says, "it read to me like a Woody Allen movie, verbatim. And I thought that was not something I should be in."

But the two do have their parallels. Both are tortured, insecure comic geniuses of Hebraic descent who changed their names and abandoned brilliant stand-up acts for film careers. Allen, however, cranks out a movie every year—some good, some bad, but like clockwork. Brooks cannot abide the "some good, some bad" thing. "I've got a minimum crap record," he says.

With maximum torment: Brooks wrestles with every decision, and usually says no. Most notoriously, he walked out on a thriving stand-up career on a night in Boston in the early seventies because he hated repeating material and didn't see comedy leading to an acting career. But there have been dozens of other, less visible refusals. Right after Michael Eisner was put in charge of programming at ABC in 1976, Brooks pitched a sitcom called *Our Man in Rattan*, in which Brooks would play a lowly TV correspondent stuck in the armpit of Africa. The deal was about to be struck when Eisner asked, "Albert, what do you see for this character in seven years?" Without missing a beat, Brooks replied, "Suicide. I don't think I'm ready to do this." He also turned down Lorne Michaels's offer to be the sole host of *Saturday Night Live.*

In movies, he's rejected countless summer comedies, from *Midnight Run* and *Dragnet* to *Sgt. Bilko.* "Some people can get away with stuff, and other people can't," Brooks explains. "Look at Tom Hanks's career. He's done some brilliant acting, he will die being respected like Jimmy Stewart. But mixed in with great stuff, he has done crap. Let's start naming them: *Bachelor Party, Dragnet, Joe Versus the Volcano.* . . . The thing with the house. But you know what? Tom Hanks is blessed, because he never seemed like he gave a shit. And when you're just an actor, you're given the leeway of making the mistake. But when you make your own movies, it's harder."

Such as when, after *Defending Your Life,* Brooks rewrote and starred in *The Scout,* an old baseball script that had been variously attached to Walter Matthau, Rodney Dangerfield, and Peter Falk. While it had its funny moments, it was clobbered by the baseball strike, and, more crucial, it frustrated and confused Brooks loyalists.

"I'm not out for quantity," Brooks says. "I mean, Stanley Kubrick will end up making a lot of movies, but one or two will be the ones he's remembered for, that changed something." And indeed, Brooks is like comedy's Kubrick, a cult figure admired by every peer and authority, but so perfectionist that his fans worry whether he'll ever make another movie. *Mother* is only Brooks's fourth film as director since his debut, *Real Life,* in 1979. Asked about how his record compares to Kubrick's, Brooks says, "I'm catching up. It's like that horse-racing game at the arcade. Every time the ball rolls over that flap, 'And Brooks passes Kubrick! And Brooks and Kubrick!'"

And surreally enough, it was Kubrick himself who persuaded Brooks not to quit the movie business altogether in 1982 after the failure of Brooks's *Modern Romance*, the harrowing tale of an obsessive, jealous man who dumps his girlfriend, grovels for her to return, then drives her away. The studio who made it, Columbia, loved it until test screenings went poorly, then demanded that Brooks add a scene in which a psychiatrist explains his character's behavior. When Brooks refused, he was told, he says, "'If you don't fix it, you won't have a second week [in theaters].' That put me into bed. I was very, very upset. Then Kubrick called me from London. He'd seen the movie, and he said, 'I've been trying to make a movie like that forever, how did you do it?' Here was the guy who made *2001*, asking me how I did something!" The two continued to correspond until the day Brooks proposed to visit Kubrick in England; Brooks says that Kubrick then muttered, "Um, that is not a good thing to do," and he never heard from him again.

Well, almost never. "One night he called me up," Brooks says, "and he said, 'Albert, I'm thinking of making a movie, and I'm wondering—what do you think of Steve Martin?' And I'm going, 'What are you doing? Ask someone else!'"

So who is Albert Brooks's mother, and why is he making a movie that may or may not be about her? Until now, Brooks followers have paid more attention to his father, radio comedian Harry Einstein, who had an alter ego known as Parkyakarkus and died on the dais of the Friars Club in 1958, just after delivering a roast of Desi Arnaz and Lucille Ball. Brooks was eleven at the time; Einstein had been ailing most of his son's life, and Brooks was raised mostly by his mother, Thelma Leeds, an actress who had met Einstein in the Milton Berle movie *New Faces of 1937* and retired to raise her sons. (Besides Cliff, there's also Bob, aka Super Dave Osborne.)

Brooks and his mother clearly love one another and speak several times a week, yet whenever he achieves anything, she seems surprised. When he was first booked on *The Tonight Show*, she marveled, "Really? Johnny'd have you on?" He wouldn't allow her to be interviewed by *Premiere*, saying, "She didn't make the movie," and that it isn't actually about her. But the real reason may be the one he gave when he turned down a similar request in 1991: "I don't want to have to go 'Oh *Maaa*' in front of all the readers of the *New York Times*."

In Brooks's script, Beatrice Henderson and her science-fiction writer son, John (another son, a successful sports agent, is played by Rob Morrow), banter almost nonstop, arguing about everything from John's decision to write a sequel to his last novel to his choice of jam. "There are two kinds of mothers in the world," says Brooks. "The one that approves of everything, and the other. And this movie is about the other."

A decade earlier, Brooks says he might have asked his mother to play Beatrice, but today she's eighty-four (and recently had a valve-replacement operation). He wanted to score a casting coup, to play opposite someone who hadn't been seen onscreen in a while.

One of his first stops was to the Reagans' house, but after some readings the former Nancy Davis told him, "This is going to kill me for the rest of my life, but I can't do this."

"She was thinking like a movie person," says Brooks's longtime collaborator Monica Johnson, who cowrote *Mother*. If Reagan had died during shooting, Johnson reasons, the movie's insurance probably wouldn't have covered the disruption caused by a state funeral. But Brooks says, "Oh God, no, it was never that literal. Imagine Nancy Reagan's position. She's still one of the most famous people in America, a former first lady, and [Ronald Reagan's] still alive and hopefully well. It was just about her leaving his side."

Scott Rudin, for one, was relieved. "I thought it was the kind of stunt that would be an interesting announcement and probably a bad movie," he says.

Brooks also went to see Doris Day, now an animal-rescue activist living in Carmel. "I've never seen so many dogs in my life," Brooks recalls. "Their heads were in every window. They all started barking—you've never lived till you've had twenty-six dogs bark at you. Scary! They live three or four to a room; they have doggie beds." Over lunch at her country club, Day turned him down. "It was interesting," he says, "because I think she reached the decision in my presence that she didn't want to be in movies anymore."

Brooks came close to casting Esther Williams, whom he'd seen on a talk show acting "very motherly." When he went to see her at her house, he found it "lovely, not ostentatious. Lots of pictures of Fernando and Lorenzo Lamas and all those people."

They rehearsed a seven-page scene in which Beatrice tries to serve John some ancient, crusted-over, off-brand ice cream out of her freezer. "Esther acted very well; she made me laugh," says Brooks. But he couldn't help noticing that inside her freezer was Häagen-Dazs. For him, this symbolized the basic difference between Williams and Beatrice. "I didn't want Esther to have to act a person that she wasn't," he says. "She's so upset—she said to somebody, 'If I didn't have Häagen-Dazs, I would've had the part!'"

The way Brooks finally found his mother was like one of those classic cornball movies where your true love is there in the room all along, you just never noticed. He'd known Debbie Reynolds most of his adult life, but only as the mom of his friend Carrie Fisher.

"I think Debbie always thought Carrie and I should get married," Brooks says. "She'd keep saying, 'Why don't you just give me the sperm, anyway, so she can have the children.'" (Carrie's reply was, "Mother, there can't be *two* neurotic parents!") Except for a cameo in Oliver Stone's *Heaven and Earth*, Reynolds hadn't acted in a movie since 1971's *What's the Matter with Helen?* Brooks didn't initially consider approaching the star of *Singin' in the Rain* and *The Unsinkable Molly Brown* because, as Johnson puts it, "Debbie was in her high Vegas period," performing nightly at her own casino-museum there.

But at eleven o'clock one night, Brooks was driving in his car and called Fisher, waking her up. "Do you think your mother could play this part?" he said.

"She'd be great," Fisher replied. She called Reynolds, and told her, "Mother, you have to fly in and read for Albert."

Reynolds balked. "'I can't leave to do a movie!'" she says she told him. "'My whole life, all my pension money is here!'" But reading the script convinced her—"It was a wonderful character and an interesting relationship"—and she hopped a plane to LA to meet with Brooks. "I went to Paramount," Reynolds recalls, "which has totally changed since I did *Rat Race* there. Now the gate's someplace else. I got lost. Then you have to park your car somewhere and walk a million miles. By the time I got up the stairs and found his office, I said, 'My God, I feel like I'm in *Lost Horizon*.' But then Albert was so casual, just like the little boy I met multiyears ago."

After they read a scene, Brooks told her, "Well, that's fine."

"What's fine?" Reynolds asked.

"Well, you have it," he said. "I'd love you to do it."

"Albert, you can't take me by one reading, you have to ask me to read another scene!"

"I don't have to," he said.

"Albert!" Reynolds cried. "I don't understand—is that how it's done today? You had me read one scene—it wasn't even the most important one—and you say I've got it?"

"Now you sound like my mother," he said.

"Oh," Reynolds said. "So I just did the other scene."

"That's right," Brooks said.

To make a movie, Reynolds had to rearrange her life. She got Mickey Rooney and the Smothers Brothers to sub for her in Vegas; she switched from going to sleep at 4 a.m. to waking at 4 a.m. "I'm a dancer," she says. "I was brought up to rehearse. Albert wrote scenes that are very active in what I call bits of business, where you cook an entire meal, so you have to rehearse it like a play. When Bette Davis and I did a cooking scene in *A Catered Affair*, we rehearsed two weeks. But Albert would run a scene twice and say, 'Okay, let's shoot it!' I almost passed out."

From Brooks's perspective, the main concern was getting Reynolds to shelve her entertainer persona and become an unassuming Sausalito grandma. But she impressed him from the start. "Before the Monday we started shooting in her character's house," he says, "she came in on the weekend, and worked in her kitchen. Nobody asked her to. Stuff Meryl used to do, you know? I saw a real actress, someone dissecting and understanding and trying to do it right. I didn't expect it, because I'd seen her for so long as a Vegas performer."

Brooks hadn't let Reynolds meet his real mom to avoid influencing her performance, but Leeds showed up on the set near the end of filming. "She's very sophisticated and intelligent, artsy—much different than I played it." And what was the dynamic between mother and son? "She told him what to do!" Reynolds says. "'You're going to put the camera over *there?*' He became a little boy of three. He put his hands behind his back and said, 'Yes, Mother. Yes, Mother.' I think Albert adores her, but I don't think that they have a relationship that's totally—they're working on it, you know what I mean?"

Even if kinks remain between him and his mother, Brooks seems quite happy these days. He has a serious girlfriend, Kimberly Shlain, an artist who created a web site for Oliver Stone called Disinformation. He recently got a call from Sidney Lumet, asking him to play a supporting role in *Critical Care*, as a sixty-five-year-old, alcoholic surgeon—and he said yes! He's learning to let go of the career perfectionism a little. "It's a combination of getting older and realizing there's a limited amount of time," Brooks says. "I don't think you want to die with just your career. I can't imagine clutching it to yourself as you're going out of this world."

The line "Nobody ever says, 'I wish I'd gone to the office more'" comes to mind, and at the mention of it Brooks nods in agreement. "Yeah, that's right," he says as his comedic brain starts clicking. "But someone *must.* Someone who got killed at *home!*" With that, he laughs heartily, having cracked up his toughest audience.

All the Choices

Gavin Smith / 1999

From *Film Comment*, July/August 1999, 14–21. Reprinted with permission from *Film Comment* and the Film Society of Lincoln Center. © *Film Comment* 1999.

In Albert Brooks's new comedy *The Muse*, a Hollywood screenwriter (played by Brooks) attempts to reignite his stalled career by employing the services of a muse (Sharon Stone, demonstrating she's an impressive comedienne). Descended from one of the seven muses of Greek myth, she boasts an impressive track record of divinely inspired careers—at one point she and Brooks bump into Rob Reiner, who exclaims, "Thank you for *The American President.*" Expensive, demanding, and capricious, the muse rapidly takes over the screenwriter's life, requiring lavish treatment and eventually moving in with Brooks and his wife (Andie MacDowell).

Cowritten by Brooks and Monica Johnson, this satire of Hollywood is embellished with sharp, frequently hilarious observation of its ritual humiliations and shallow social and professional interactions, with notable contributions from Jeff Bridges as a self-absorbed Oscar-winning screenwriter friend, Steven Wright as Stan Spielberg ("I'm Steven's cousin"), and Martin Scorsese in a self-parodying cameo. But at its core is the spectacle of a rational, down-to-earth individual who, faced with a career crisis that threatens the life of comfortable domestic affluence he has built for himself, succumbs with surprisingly few misgivings to an absurd New Age fix, and gets more than he bargained for.

At heart *The Muse* is less a broadside against the industry than another of Brooks's subtly offbeat cautionary comedies of modern anxiety. Once again, a Me Generation everyman occupies an ideal lifestyle or system, blissfully unaware of its underlying precariousness. Whether it be the callow filmmaker's perfect experiment in documentary in *Real Life* (1979), the impossible fantasy of "true love" in *Modern Romance* (1981), the way a life of complacent materialism is exchanged for an equally deluded freedom of the road in the anti-Reagan-zeitgeist *Lost in America* (1985), or ended altogether by the ultimate bummer of sudden

death at the start of *Defending Your Life* (1991), the Brooks protagonist is oblivious until too late. In *The Muse*, as in *Mother* (1996) and *Lost in America*, the
great central comic conceit is his adoption of an improbable radical solution:
when your marriage fails, move back in with your mother to figure out why your
relationships with women don't work; when you don't get the promotion you
feel you deserve, quit, drop out of society, and go on the road to find yourself; if
your writing career goes south, hire a muse and do whatever she instructs, even
if you can't shake the feeling you're being shortchanged.

The striking consistency of Brooks's comic vision is reinforced by the char-
acteristic strategies he deploys. Almost every film is essentially a two-character
piece in which Brooks pairs himself with an actress in an unstable or artificial,
often domestic situation; *The Muse* diverges from this scenario, if only through
triangulation—this time Brooks give himself two female leads to contend with—
but still avoids the obvious. Instead of finding himself torn between two women,
Brooks typically must endure the humiliation of being sidelined as his muse-
for-hire bonds with his wife and inspires her to launch a line of home-baked
cookies that win instant acclaim.

Brooks's protagonists tend to be successful yet average creative types who
write or work in advertising or filmmaking (one of the incidental joys of *Modern
Romance* is its dead-accurate depiction of a film editor's working life). His char-
acterizations effectively refract the contradictions, compromises, and neuroses
of the Baby Boom generation with its overdeveloped sense of entitlement and
unapologetic materialism: narcissistic and controlling yet insecure and resigned,
reflexively self-analytical yet lacking emotional self-honesty. It's hard to think of
another American filmmaker who has dedicated him/herself so completely to
scrutinizing the foibles of his generational peers without becoming moralistic
or sentimental.

This pattern of structuring comedy around a distinct personality-type is
also evident in Brooks's early work. His early seventies comedy bits for TV, two
unique records, *Comedy Minus One* (1973) and *A Star is Bought* (1975), and his
six short films for *Saturday Night Live* in 1975–76 all emanate from a specific
comic persona: smugly self-confident, oblivious to its own absurdity. This holds
true from the early comic routines that established him, presenting supremely
assured yet inept performers (a loquacious French mime, a ventriloquist whose
mouth moves), through to his first feature, *Real Life*, the zenith of this mode. In
formal terms an extension of Brooks *SNL* shorts, this mock-documentary parody
of PBS's landmark *An American Family* pushes the arrogance and narcissism of
its main character to the point of implosion. Brooks's next film, Kubrick favorite
Modern Romance, a truly terrifying comedy of obsessive jealousy and loss of
control, signaled a decisive aesthetic shift toward a narrative approach based in

more dimensional character and psychology. Brooks's subsequent films (and even a number of his performances for other directors, notably in James L. Brooks's *Broadcast News* and *I'll Do Anything*) are defined by the more complex experience of humbling misfortune and an ensuing struggle to overcome pervasive anxiety and regain existential terra firma.

While a cult of personality has deservedly formed around his compact oeuvre, the reductive perception of Brooks as merely preoccupied with neurosis erases any distance between Brooks and the characters he plays, and has more than once cued the glib tag of "a West Coast Woody Allen." But his work has none of the latter's self-regarding pretension, misanthropic cynicism, and self-pity. Moreover, it displays a formal integrity that has entirely eluded the ever-derivative Allen. Brooks's distinctive filmmaking style is remarkably discreet and unemphatic; he has a light, deft touch, with a classical precision and economy, shooting and cutting his scenes in smooth, seamless successions of medium shots, with clean, high-key lighting. ("A style so distanced and disciplined it can only be termed analytical," wrote J. Hoberman.) He also knows how to take his time; if you look at *Mother* you see scenes that last as long as ten minutes, and you're never impatient to move on.

But perhaps because of his relatively sparse directorial output—six films in twenty years—even some of Brooks's critical champions have called him an underachiever. I know what they mean. Brooks seems constitutionally incapable of going over the top, and he's not interested in blowing the audience away. In his elusive sui generis brand of antisentimental, observational comedy, the comic possibilities of character and situation are always restrained by a defining sense of plausible reality and authentic, self-revealing emotional experience. This places him completely at odds with American comedy's currently prevailing aesthetic—a parodic, cartoonish absurdism, fed on high energy, outrageous excess, and mock sentimentality—whose prime exponents include Jim Carrey, the Farrelly brothers, Ben Stiller, and the post–*Saturday Night Live* Adam Sandler and Mike Meyers.

That he stands outside this mainstream is ironic indeed, since the rise of Brooks and peers like Steve Martin and Andy Kaufman in the early seventies signaled the emergence of an oppositional sensibility that began to gradually displace the dominant postwar comedy establishment. "Jokes are disappearing," said Brooks, the son of a member of the old school of stand-up, and in their place he installed a more conceptual kind of humor. It was apt that he was referred to as a "comedian's comedian," because he practiced a unique, at the time innovative brand of self-reflexive metacomedy that dismantled the familiar, seemingly moribund comedy formats—ventriloquism, impression, stand-up itself. And just as his first short film *Albert Brooks' Famous School for Comedians* (1972) and the subsequent *SNL* shorts pressed ahead in the same vein, targeting TV and documentary, one of the not-so-incidental pleasures of Brooks's films is their sustained, sardonic commentary on the ubiquity of movies and their illusions in his characters' lives. *Lost in America,* a film that opens with Rex Reed being interviewed by Larry King about what's wrong with today's movies, epitomizes this, with its yuppie couple's recurrent recourse to *Easy Rider* as a blueprint for the rest of their lives, and its casting of director Garry Marshall (who is superb) as an amused, all-business Vegas casino manager. In *The Muse,* the Los Angeles-born-and-bred Brooks returns to the ground zero of movie-made America, resuming his interrogation of the emotional life and values of his generation as it navigates treacherous waters.

Gavin Smith: Are you sticking your neck out with this film, a story about someone who faces rejection in Hollywood?

Albert Brooks: I guess since that's what I've always done, it doesn't feel so much like sticking my neck out. I've never come from a safe place. I sort of began my whole comedy career sticking my neck out. So I don't know any better. Hopefully, I'm always going to be honest enough with what I do where I can leave my neck out. I just don't consciously think in terms of safe and unsafe.

GS: You don't feel there's a pattern in your work of exploring specific fears?

AB: I think I do. I think that's the nature of writing. I don't think it would be fun to do it otherwise. Unless you do that, it doesn't get exciting. I've never made a sequel; I've never gone to a place that was familiar to me. I had seen lots of different movies about this town, and those scenes, to me, don't ring true. The people I've seen in other movies, cast as studio people or agents, they're just not what I believe is really there. I wanted a chance to put my two cents in. Casting Mark Feuerstein as opposed to Martin Short as the studio executive makes a big difference. I try not to do these parts in a clichéd way; I at least try to make them real enough that you don't even have to know about the business to know it's real.

GS: Why is your work more rooted in realism than most current comedy?

AB: Well, I didn't think about it like, I'll do this and they'll do that. I once had an agent say to me, years ago . . . we were having some discussion over an argument about a studio project and he said, "Gee, I don't know why you always take the hard road," and I said, "You think I see two roads?" You don't really analyze what you do—you just do what you're able to do, and if you stick around long enough, then maybe you'll start your own category or you'll fit into a category.

When I started, one of the first things I ever did was *The Dean Martin Summer Show.* The producer, after seeing one spot, gave me eight shows, and said to me, "Do you have material?" I said, "Yes," and I really didn't, and he said, "Okay, you'll start in four weeks." And I went home and figured out what kind of comedian I would be, and I came back and I showed him my stuff, and he said to me, "You know what? If you do this kind of material you're going to have trouble your whole life, because you're ten feet above the audience." I said, "I don't know what you're talking about—this is all I know how to do," and he took this long pause and he said, "Okay, that was all I wanted to hear. Go do it." You just do what you know. Some people are right in the mainstream from the get-go. They don't ever have a problem with that, that's just who they are.

GS: What inspired the film?

AB: The idea of something or somebody that is going to sit on your shoulder and guide you through this stuff. It's so romantic and, obviously, it's such an important part of the history of creativity, this idea of a creative guardian angel. The movie certainly tells you that it's really in your own head if you believe that it's true. I just always liked that idea that there was an outside party that could contribute to the success of a creative project. It's also the idea that Hollywood will embrace anybody and do it quickly. People rise up in this town very fast, and sometimes they're even criminals, let alone not who they say they are.

GS: Do you think the character you play is a good screenwriter?

AB: I think he's a good screenwriter going through the exact period that tons of screenwriters are. Ninety-nine percent of writers write for somebody. There's only a few people in life who ever get to write because they want to and people come to them. Most people write for hire. As those people get older, I think they all get a little scared when the executives become younger than their children; they get a little worried that they're not going to get those jobs anymore, so they start writing things that maybe they don't love or they're not close to. I think that's sort of what Steven Phillips is. . . .

GS: The distance between the character and you is probably greater than it's been in any of your other films.

AB: People always like to think everything's you. I used to answer this question a lot—"*Lost in America*, is it you?" and I said, "I don't own a motorhome, I've never lost all my money in Las Vegas, I've never worked for an ad agency, but sure, why not?" I'm not interesting enough on my own that you'd want to see a film about me. My whole interest comes alive after I create something and can get it on its feet. Why would you want to see me sit in a room all day trying to do that? That's what Albert Brooks does.

GS: But there is a kind of unspoken contract between you and the audience: you create something imaginary in its circumstances and they'll believe it's you up there.

AB: I understand what you're saying, but let's go back to somebody like Jack Benny, one of the greatest radio and early television comedians that ever lived. The reason why he was so brilliant was that he did nothing. He would have these long, forty-second takes where he would just stare. But the audience knew him so well that they laughed at those silences. He was known as someone who was cheap, the most frugal, he never paid his employees; this is what people roared at. One of the biggest laughs in the history of radio is: Jack Benny's walking home late at night and a guy comes out of an alley and says, "Your money or your life." And Benny doesn't say anything. And the audience starts laughing and finally the guy says, "*Your money or your life!*" and Benny goes, "I'm thinking it over!"

His whole life, Jack Benny faced this: "Are you really that cheap?" And Jack Benny was one of the most charitable men that ever lived. These older comedians all played their own name. So it got confusing. I'm the last one to look at these characters that I play as being me. I've always hated the word *neurotic*—life is not an easy road for anybody no matter who you are, so all I'm really doing is saying, "Look what happens."

When I was a kid, 99 percent of the stand-up comedians just did jokes that had nothing to do with them and you could call them everyman jokes. I don't know where it happened, but as stand-up comedy changed over the years, everyman changed to individual man, and that's when I started. When I played Albert Brooks in *Real Life* I learned how confusing that gets, because people didn't know me very well then. I was reading reviews like, "This Albert Brooks should never be allowed to make another film, and he doesn't know how to handle a family. How dare he be so rough with children." And I'm going, "Holy shit, don't people get it?" So unless you play something so bizarre and unrealistic, you're always going to get mixed up with your work, which is just the way it is.

I would not have made *Modern Romance* unless I had that kind of trouble in my life with breaking up. I didn't do it as much as that character, but I did it enough to be able to write and do that, so for comedic purposes, I take behavior that I might do and I square it. And then you have a performance, you have a movie. You have to be fearless about it, you can't go, "Oh gee, am I gonna come off too this or too that?" Don't make the movie then, don't do that subject if that's what you're afraid of; play a lovable teddy bear. If I think about my next film and think, "This could be very embarrassing, I would never do it," you have to commit yourself to the part. If you don't do that, you have no chance of ever doing it great. I really did feel when *Real Life* came out that people would automatically go, "Oh, is he brilliant, the way he played that character with his own name." And I was really surprised when that didn't happen. I saved the review that said, "Why would Paramount give this idiot the money to do such an important experiment?"

GS: Which of your characters is the closest to you, or the least removed?

AB: They all had distances and they all had similarities. Maybe that's too much of a safe answer, but it's really true. I don't think I could play a character that I didn't have something in common with. Maybe when I made *Modern Romance*

I was closest to that kind of feeling than other feelings—no, I don't even think that's true. When I did *Defending Your Life*, I was very consumed with the idea of fear and not being afraid. I still think about that subject. I think I'm equally invested in every movie.

GS: So the movies reflect what's going on in you and preoccupying you.

AB: Yes, but because movies take so long to make, [often] by the time the movie comes out you've dealt with that issue already.

GS: That must be weird.

AB: It *is* weird. It's working in a time machine. When I went through that behavior that the character went through in *Modern Romance*, I was probably seventeen, I wasn't able to make movies then. But the behavior was so strong and interesting and weird that I stuffed it away so I could write about it.

When I made that movie, the studio had seen it lots of times with an audience and they seemed to be fine, they were treating me nicely. Then they went up to San Francisco and tested it, and they just hated what they got, they didn't like these scores. And they treated me as if I had just made another movie than the one I had been showing them. They kept saying to me, "Add a psychiatrist scene," and I said, "Why?" And they said, "Explain that behavior, they don't understand what's wrong with him—listen to these cards: he's got a beautiful girl, a Porsche, what's his problem?" I said, "You know what, I'm not being facetious, I don't know his problem. I can't explain it, I didn't write the movie as a philosopher, I just wrote it as someone showing the behavior." Now today I could give you that answer. I know, this many years later, why people act like that. But I didn't know that then. And they just thought I was being an asshole.

GS: Do you think the dialogue in your recent films reflects a more therapy-oriented sensibility?

AB: I can't disagree with that. But that's just getting smarter. It's not something you leave in, or leave out on purpose. I just knew that one day I needed to write *Mother*, just having conversations with my own mother for my whole life, I just found it so interesting, and I had never seen that put on film in that fashion.

GS: Mother-son relationships tend to be depicted as somehow unhealthy, as in *The Manchurian Candidate* or *Psycho*.

AB: Or they're weird, they're like John Candy and Maureen O'Hara. I wanted an experience where I would go, "Oh my God, that's my mother, that's my mother's house, that's my mother's kitchen, and I knew I wasn't the only one." That movie had to have been more intellectualized than, say, *Real Life*, just in order to make it. The point of that movie, for that son to be able to reach a point where he could let his mother off the hook, that did need to be figured out. That's why people go to shrinks. So I did it in an hour and a half where normally it would take you fifteen years.

GS: I've read that you've always had a fascination with technology and science. In a number of your films, your characters come up with a perfect system or plan to solve their problems.

AB: In *The Muse* it's, "How do I get this person into my life to make everything okay?" Maybe in some unconscious way, I'm trying to put order to disorder. I've never said it that way before, but to me, that's funny. How do you order something that is not to be ordered, how do you try to regiment your life where it's not supposed to be? The people who get into the biggest trouble are the ones who set up their cards the most careful—those are the cards that fall the fastest. So here's a comedy character saying, "If I do A, B, and C, I'll get D," but he always gets F. In *Lost in America*, sitting down with [Julie Hagerty], telling her what it's going to be like if we have fifty-four grand and we do this and do that, it's like a little computer spewing out these answers.

GS: How do you think your filmmaking has evolved since you began?

AB: You can't work at anything and not get a style, otherwise you'd be insane. You have to learn that there's no way to make your first film your third film. You just don't know what you don't know. I've learned how to do things for a budget. There was a time when I started to shoot with two cameras to speed things up. I just understand the constraints I've been given. I've learned about who to hire to help me, what kind of a crew I need to make it go fast and pleasant. It takes a while to learn the other crafts enough so that you can be intelligent about it. The first movie you ever do, if the cinematographer tells you he needs six hours to light a room and that's all there is to it, you have nothing to compare to. Then when you see Michael Ballhaus do it in ten minutes and it looks brilliant, you now don't accept that any longer. That's the hardcore part of filmmaking.

GS: There's a real sense of control and ease in how you cover scenes. It doesn't feel as though you do lots of setups; you seem to know what you want.

AB: Yes, I do. There's a couple of scenes in *The Muse* that I'm really proud of because they're exquisitely simple. When Sharon Stone and Andie MacDowell have that first lunch together, that's one very slow move; it starts on one side of the table, featuring one of the characters a little bit and moves to the other. It was designed that way, we worked hard to make it that way, that was important to me. I think I have a style I am very intent on—I've always sort of imagined movies as people looking through a window. Sort of peeping in on the goings-on. So unless it's for a comedic effect, I don't make the camera the star.

GS: In scenes in restaurants or public places, you'll cut to a single of an incidental character like a waiter or a store clerk for a moment, giving emphasis to someone we never see again.

AB: I think that's one of the most fun parts of movies. One of the best reviews of *Lost in America* I got was from Pauline Kael; she said the little characters that come and go in his movie are like candy for the audience. I love little characters. The more interesting they can be, the better.

GS: So the casting process must be a really important part of directing for you.

AB: It's absolutely crucial. One of the funniest scenes in *The Muse* is the Italian guy in the Spago party [Mario Opinato]. There was only so much I could write. So I saw forty people who had dialects, and sat in my office with them and tried to play. And this was the one guy who never dropped the ball. Whatever I asked him, he came back at me, and I just knew something could happen. And when we go there—that was multiple cameras—we just went. Generally I don't like to ad-lib in movies. If the opportunity arises and you have somebody who's capable, you can maybe take off a little bit from [the script]. But what never works is where you don't know where to go and you start to make it up—it *looks* made up. In this case, this guy was just wonderful. Any ball I threw him, he just threw it back.

GS: When you're casting a role that's going to play opposite you, do you read with the actors?

AB: Absolutely. People say, "How can you direct yourself if you act?" Well, there's one aspect of it that's easier, because you're right there looking into their eyes. If it's false, you can tell as an actor it's not going. That's one thing that makes one director different from another. That's all it really is, is how you feel that person should be, how I feel that person should be, how Jim Carrey feels that person should be.

GS: Another question about cinematic style: you favor a consistently sweeping, symphonic score that is not particularly fashionable.

AB: Well, I'm a musical person and I have these notes in my head. I gave Elton John [composer of *The Muse*'s score] a temp score of classical music, which I never gave any other composer before. I always like the juxtaposition—trying to do the film with the action and characters as real seeming as they could be, and then cushion it in a sort of a classical musical sense with more of a timeless movie feel to it.

GS: Is it ironic?

AB: I don't know that it's irony, but it might be.

GS: In *Real Life*, when the psychology consultant quits, suddenly this music comes in. Up until then we've been watching the film as it's being shot, but at that moment we realize that the film has been edited and even scored. The director is in the cutting room making decisions.

AB: I had a lot of scenes in *Real Life* that never got in the movie and one of them was a scene with me and Mort Lindsey talking about what the [score] would be. I was sitting in an office with him and I had pictures of [Charles] Grodin up on the wall and he was at the piano looking at Grodin trying to come up with a theme, and I kept saying, "That's no good, that's no good, that's too sad."

GS: How did you meet your writing collaborator Monica Johnson, and how do you work together?

AB: She was familiar with my stand-up, and Penny Marshall was friends with both of us, and [Monica] said, "I want to meet this guy," and we hit it off. And except for *Defending Your Life*, I've been working with her ever since. We sit together, I talk into a tape recorder, so I do the main babbling and Monica will throw in anything that she thinks of, say something in a way she wants to say it. *Modern Romance* we wrote in a car, with a tape recorder on. I'm the one who's doing the primary; I play all the parts and the stage direction and Monica has all the ideas and lines she can think of. She provides this place where comedy can live, she's very muse-like in that sense. From the very beginning, when you talk about the Albert Brooks character, she's understood that character very innately. Not me, him. She understands that guy very well. It was a challenge for me to do it without her, it was harder. It's much nicer to work with somebody, it's more fun.

GS: So you're each other's first audience?

AB: Yes, absolutely. In other words, I know if I can't make Monica laugh it won't go any further than that.

GS: Do you have a sense of what need your work satisfies in you?

AB: Well, up until recently, when I found my wife and I had a child, it was almost the only thing I had. And I don't know what else I would have been or why I'm even living if not. I just had to get all this stuff out. From the beginning, especially if you're funny from such a young age, you almost have to do it or you go insane.

GS: Did being considered a prodigy and comic genius create pressure?

AB: It's a great thing and it can be a burden. If you get clogged up with that shit, you can be in bad trouble. The worst thing that can happen to anybody trying to be creative is to feel, "Oh my God, I'm not living up to something." To me, the people that seem to be rewarded the most, who are in creative work, are the people who stay in the longest. Just stick in there and keep doing and doing. I turned down four movies that Tom Hanks took early in our careers, including *Bachelor Party* and *Dragnet*. I was there going, "Oh my God, my reputation, I can't do that." I don't think Tom Hanks thought like that, and you can't be in a better place in terms of respect than he is right now. So if you do get bogged down with who you are, it's not good.

GS: Was there a point when that did get on top of you?

AB: Yes. Absolutely. I still feel it. I still make my decisions based on somebody I want to respect. There was a time where television was the worst thing you could ever do. That doesn't seem to be true anymore, and many of the things that I still hold on to, quite frankly, I don't even think are true. Bu they're still true for me. I was trying to live up to something that I wanted to be. But you have to do that to have a career that you are proud of. It's unhealthy where it keeps you from doing something you might have fun at. You can make some mistakes and have fun doing them, and you're gonna turn out okay. But there was a time in my life where I thought if I made one mistake it was one mistake too many.

One experience that really taught me a lot was *The Scout* (1994). Monica and I rewrote this script. Then what we wrote ended in a completely different way. It did not end like *Rocky*, with that bullshit big ending. The way that movie ended was, he was taken down to the field, he threw one pitch, and the movie was over. He just was able to let the ball go. It was a very gentle, quiet moment, where you just knew that kid was going to be all right. And the studio made Michael Ritchie put on this ending, and I got so upset. They tested it with both endings, and it tested nine points higher with the phony ending. I remember I was doing the press junket in New York and the *Times* said, "Albert Brooks should be ashamed, it's the worst ending." I'm happy that was the only one of those in my life.

GS: Why didn't you direct *The Scout*?

AB: I didn't want to. I really only did *The Scout* because I just wanted to play that part, I liked that character, a guy who traveled around—it was like *Death of a Salesman*. I didn't want to direct a baseball movie. A lonely type of guy to play, but I guess it was the first at-bat. That script was originally written for Rodney Dangerfield; it was lying around, never going to get made, and I said I would like to do that. And that sort of got it alive, and then it really needed a rewrite because it was written very silly. It had no reality to it at all. It's very rare that artists get to hold out for what they want. I got spoiled. Even if it meant I couldn't make an expensive movie, or I couldn't make them as often as I want, there's no movie with my name on it that I am not proud of and cannot say this is the way I wanted it to be.

GS: Does it seem to you now that directing was always the natural destination for you?

AB: I still like to act. I enjoy acting in projects that I don't direct. Basically, I wound up directing because I could never find anybody else to do it. From the very beginning it was clear to me that my comedy had to get me to do it. If I gave *Real Life* to Carl Reiner it wouldn't have been *Real Life*, it would have been another movie. That's what directing is. Directing is simply all the choices, and if I think you're the best person to play [a part] and the other director thinks Brad Pitt's the best person, well there's the different movie right there. So it starts there and goes to every decision there is. Should he live in a two-story house? No! He should live in a bad apartment. So you've got to do it. It forces you. And certainly, once I wrote, I had to direct. If I never wrote a word, I never would have been a director. It's carrying out the instructions correctly, and it would have been way more frustrating standing on the side going, "Oh, don't do it like that!" On *The Scout*, I never told Michael Ritchie what to do, but there were many times where I had to leave because I thought, "Gee, I wouldn't have Brendan [Fraser] do it that way." But, that wasn't my job and I'm not that kind of a person. I don't butt in like that.

GS: If you had to give up two of them, which one would you keep: acting, directing, writing?

AB: If I had to, if I was forced, like it was Russia? I feel I would like to keep acting. That's the way I feel right now, but I don't want to give up any of them. I feel I'm entering an age where there's a shitload of parts that I could really play, and I'd like to keep doing that. Now, talk to me in a year. The hardest of the three is writing. It's the most gratifying; also the toughest. I would act in someone else's movie, I might even direct a movie that I hadn't written, but I'd never write a movie and that would be it. That I just wouldn't do. It would be too difficult.

GS: Given that, does your talent as a whole lie in your writing side or your performing?

AB: I know when I'm writing, I'm acting out the different people, so I would say my acting ability has helped everything. And the reason actors like working for me as a director is that I do really understand what they do and they feel comfortable. I'm not looking at them like, "Who are you and why do you get paid so much?"

GS: So writing and directing are manifestations of yourself as a performer.

AB: If there were fifty great parts for me when I was twenty or twenty-five, I probably never would have done this, but out of necessity I had to do it. I wasn't getting anything. If I was able to get a lot of work as a young actor, I never would have had the discipline to write and direct.

GS: Before you began your comedy career, you aspired to be a serious actor and studied acting at Carnegie Mellon. Why did you go in that direction when it was already established that you had this natural gift for making people laugh?

AB: In that era, the late sixties, there was nobody in stand-up; the profession of stand-up was just Vegas and cigars and the Friars Club and Sheckie Green—it wasn't a cool thing to do. If you wanted to work, you had to go work and live in Vegas. My father was a famous radio comedian, and I had certainly seen that part of it. I just didn't have any fascination or desire to do stand-up comedy. I always wanted to act, and at Carnegie I got a lot of shows my freshman year. I left after a year and a half. I also went to LA City College for a year and did the same thing.

GS: What particularly stayed with you?

AB: There was a guy named Tom Hill who taught the most wonderful thing of all, and that was the economy of acting. We get back to Jack Benny and how less is more. That always made a lot of sense to me.

GS: What happened when you returned to LA?

AB: I came back here and tried to get work, and I was nineteen and nobody at nineteen was getting much acting. Whenever a part would come up, Richard Dreyfuss would get it. I had this man at the William Morris office who has basically been in my life ever since, Herb Nanas, and I'd always go and make these people laugh. One of my friends, Larry Bishop, whose father was Joey Bishop, had a ventriloquist doll hanging around. I picked it up and one thing led to another and I created Danny and Dave, and it made everyone laugh. These people convinced me—and they said, "Listen, if you'll be willing to be funny, you'll get everything you ever want, you will zoom right past everybody else and get right to the front of the casting door." Well, I didn't. All I did was get a lot of stand-up comedy work. I probably got *Taxi Driver* because Marty Scorsese was a fan of my comedy. But it took too long to get that one part.

I started in reverse. I did all of my starting on national television. I'd think up these bits, I'd go down to *The Dean Martin Show* or *Ed Sullivan* and do it for the first time, and then after three or four years of that, I put together an hour and opened for Neil Diamond. So, I went the opposite way.

GS: How would you characterize the comic sensibility that you shared in and helped shape?

AB: I think the answer is that it was acting comedy. It was taking what I really wanted to do and putting it in the stand-up world. I would play these characters. Most of your stand-up comedians were not actors—they were joke tellers. On my first record, *Comedy Minus One*, one side of it was twenty-five minutes from my stand-up act that I was currently doing, and that was talking to the audience. But on television I would never do that. I certainly wasn't going to do "Two Jews walk into a bar," so I started out satirizing show business, the very bullshit part of show business that I hated. I did these entertainers that were terrible at it and didn't know it. That's the whole nature of making fun of the beast, to punch it in the mouth and see where it goes. You do it to tear it down. There were guys my age, and there still are people who are twenty years old, who can stand up with a cigar and tell jokes. That will never go away.

GS: When you acted in *Taxi Driver*, did you have any idea how it would turn out?

AB: No, I really didn't. I had waited so long to make a start that I would come up to Marty occasionally and say, "Do you think this is going to help me as an actor?" I think it's very rare that people who wind up doing something that lasts have an idea of that, because if you do have an idea of that, then you're sort of out of the moment.

GS: I'd heard that your role was expanded once you started working.

AB: It wasn't even there. One of the funniest lines anyone's ever said to me was at the wrap party. Paul Schrader comes up to me and says, "I just wanted to thank you. This was the one guy I didn't know." I'm thinking, "Jesus Christ, you've got a movie filled with murderers and pimps, all I'm doing is working in a campaign office—*this* is the guy you didn't know?!" The way we worked (I don't know if Marty continues to work like this) was, we would improvise during rehearsals and he would tape those. Then he would commit the best of that to the script and that's what he would shoot. So, he really didn't like you making it up the day the camera was rolling. It occurred to me that if you work in a campaign office, one of the things that would be your job is to get boxes of twenty thousand buttons. So I made up this phone conversation about the "We Are the People" badges and being upset.

GS: What contribution did you make to shaping your character in *Broadcast News*?

AB: The arc of the character was pretty clear as written: this character needed to have a catastrophic moment where he failed, [but] in the early stages Jim was not sure what should happen. I had that luxury of talking to Jim as he was writing, which is a great thing if you can do that with the writer. I remember, at 11:30 at night, seeing this man on CNN have that flop sweat experience, and I called up Jim and said, "Turn on the television!" So that was sort of how the sweating happened.

GS: What about your work in *I'll Do Anything*?

AB: I wish you could have seen the musical [version]. That was the greatest thing in the world, and it broke my heart that the movie came out like it did. The irony of that movie is, the very thing it was about is what it succumbed to. I mean, here's a movie whose whole being is about testing and succumbing to the testing, and that's exactly what happened to Jim. I understand why, but the ambition was so great, if he had stuck to it, in my opinion, it certainly wouldn't have done any worse, and in the long run it would have been a really important movie.

GS: Did you do a good job with the singing and dancing?

AB: You weren't going to buy my albums and make out to them, but I was sort of in the Rex Harrison vein. I sold a song and I did it within the character. I had the title song, "I'll Do Anything." People were lined up to see the preview of that terrible movie that my character produced, and he was going up and down the line singing, "I'll do anything to make you like me." And then there was a song called "There is Lonely," after he got the opening weekend grosses; it was so funny to sing that kind of song to that subject. We worked a solid year. As I look back, I got to study with Twyla Tharp, who did the choreography. Where would I have ever gotten that chance? That was a thrill.

GS: Is it true your character was modeled on producer Joel Silver?

AB: Well, he never spoke to me again, so it must have been.

Albert Brooks

Joe Rhodes / 1999

From *Us*, September 1999, 48–51. Reprinted with permission.

Many folks in Hollywood say that he's the funniest man alive. But, compared with Jim Carrey's or Adam Sandler's, his movies don't make a dime. Now, on the eve of his new film, *The Muse*, the writer-director-actor sounds off on life as a Hollywood outsider, fatherhood and the art of doing comedy that doesn't "stop up your brain."

Strange stories about Albert Brooks have surfaced over the years. Most of them involve houses. There is the one about the house he lived in that no one was allowed to enter. If, for example, you needed to send a package to him, he would reportedly ask you to leave it outside his front gate. He would then wait, and when the coast was clear, run out, silent-movie style, and snatch up the package. Then there was the time he invited a journalist into his new abode. When the reporter wrote that the decor of one room was "dark," Brooks was supposedly so crushed by the criticism that he banned the press from his home forever.

Of course, it's not such a stretch to imagine Albert Brooks saddled with an overabundance of neuroses. This, after all, is the man who nervously spewed sweat as a substitute anchorman in 1987's *Broadcast News*. And the films he has written, directed, and starred in often give you the sense that you're watching Brooks's deepest anxieties play out onscreen. In *Defending Your Life* (1991), with Meryl Streep, his character dies in a car crash, but before he can be sent to heaven, he is put on trial to determine if he is worthy to enter paradise; in *Mother* (1996), he plays a twice-divorced man who moves in with his overbearing mom (Debbie Reynolds) so he can get to the root of his troubles with women.

His new movie, *The Muse*, which costars Jeff Bridges, Andie MacDowell, and Sharon Stone, travels equally touchy terrain. Brooks portrays a screenwriter who is told by a young, weaselly studio executive that, possibly, writing is something he shouldn't do anymore. Brooks then goes on a desperate hunt for inspiration, which he finds in the form of an actual muse (played by Stone).

In fact, the fear of coming up empty creatively has dogged Brooks for years. "One of the most famous routines I ever did as a stand-up was about running out of material," he says, referring to a legendary *Tonight Show* appearance in the early 1970s in which he glumly stared at the audience for a while before dropping his trousers, painting a face on his bare chest, hitting himself with a pound cake, breaking eggs over his head, and then, shamefaced, declaring, "This isn't the real me." As he says, "Obviously that stuff was in the back of my mind."

And what a strange and complex mind it is—a bit too complicated, at times, for mass-market consumption. Of the movies Brooks has directed, the most financially successful was *Mother*, and that made a mere nineteen million dollars. But, says Stone, "That's part of his genius. He understands that not everybody gets him. And he doesn't care."

Since his birth on July 22, 1947, Albert Brooks has been a punch line of sorts. He was named Albert Einstein, a little postnatal humor courtesy of his father, the late Harry Einstein (the Greek-dialect radio comedian known to his fans as Parkyakarkus), and his mother, Thelma, a former actress. Brooks grew up in Beverly Hills, California, the youngest of three sons. (One brother, Cliff, is an advertising executive; the other, Bob, is the crash-prone stunt comic Super Dave Osborne.) When Brooks was eleven years old, his father died, and he started spending most of his time at the house of his best friend, Rob Reiner (who would grow up to play Meathead on *All in the Family* and direct movies like *The Princess Bride*). In some ways, Reiner's father, Carl, became a surrogate dad to Brooks. Carl was amazed by Albert's prodigious comedic gifts and declared once on *The Tonight Show* that the two funniest people he'd ever seen were Mel Brooks and this high-school kid named Albert Einstein.

In many ways, the statement was prophetic. Brooks honed his skills as a stand-up comic by working in nightclubs, then made his television stand-up debut on *The Steve Allen Show* in 1967. Throughout the 1970s, his no-punch-line appearances on *The Tonight Show*, in which he'd do bits about incompetent ventriloquists or mimes who wouldn't shut up, invariably left Johnny Carson bent double at his desk, gasping for air. In 1975, when Lorne Michaels asked Brooks to be the permanent host of *Saturday Night Live*, Brooks, typically iconoclastic, chose instead to contribute a series of six short movies. In one of them, he plays a filmmaker who is talking about his work when his young, attention-seeking daughter walks by and bites him on the hand. He calls for a cop to take her away, then says nonchalantly, "You won't be seeing her again."

"What frustrates me most in terms of people appreciating Albert," says Rob Reiner, "is people still haven't seen him in his best element, which is free form in a room, when his mind is just working. What I've proposed for many years— and maybe if you print it, he'll do it—is that Albert and I just sit down and talk to each other for a couple of weeks and film the whole thing. It would be like *My Dinner with Andre*, except it would be *My Lunch with Albert*."

Today, there is little sign of the man who once would accept packages only outside his front gate. Sitting in his office on the Universal Studios lot (part of his production deal with October Films), he leans back in his chair, puts his black shoes on the desk, and sighs comfortably. The place looks as if it's still being moved into, even though Brooks has been here for more than a year. There are boxes in corners, half-painted walls, and not much furniture. The only adornment is a lonely poster from *Taxi Driver*, his feature-film debut. There are no personal pictures, no trinkets, hardly anything to indicate the new and more mellow Albert Brooks.

After settling in for a lifetime of bachelorhood, Brooks reconsidered his status in late 1995, when mutual friends introduced him to Kimberly Shlain, now thirty-three, an artist who owns and runs her own website design firm. They married in March 1997, and their first child, Jacob, was born in October 1998.

His family may be part of the reason for his calm. Throughout the conversation, Brooks shows shades of the characters he so often creates: a little insecure, sometimes exasperated, and, even, yes, funny. But for the most part, he appears relaxed. Until you notice the paper clip he has had in his hand for the entire interview, which he has slowly twisted into a tight, worried knot.

Joe Rhodes: You've been fairly public about your view that film comedy has become, essentially, one big fart joke, and that certain comics—Adam Sandler, for one—have cheated themselves and the audience by always going for the lowest common denominator. Why does this bother you so much?

Albert Brooks: Comedy is like eating, you know? You eat a lot of McDonald's hamburgers, and you like them until somebody says, "You know what? Maybe I can give you a full meal with a little bit of vegetables, and I can make you like that, too." And before you know it, you're eating something that's not stopping up your heart. It's the same thing with your brain. This stuff stops up your brain. People just don't know it.

JR: So it's like cerebral sclerosis?

AB: Exactly. That's what it is. It's fine to have fast food comedy, but it shouldn't be the only kind. That's all I'm saying. Vary your diet. Treat your sense of humor like your heart. Keep it flowing, keep it lean. Keep it smart.

JR: So, it bothers you that Adam Sandler gets twenty million dollars a picture for making potty jokes, and you're struggling just to get your movies made?

AB: You know what, I don't begrudge Adam Sandler anything. I just think that if people could get a little bit of choice, they'd take it. They'd say, "Maybe an hour and a half of the fart joke is too much. How about just an hour, and give me something else for that other thirty minutes?" I tell you, my biggest fear is that I die and I go to heaven and God says, "Did you hear the one about the two guys who crapped on the lawn?" Have you heard from Sandler about any of this? No. He wouldn't know me to call me. I don't think he would care, anyway. And he shouldn't.

JR: You've always lived in Hollywood, and yet you've never really fit in. What has that been like?

AB: To be Hollywood is not geographical. You could live in Chicago and still be Hollywood. But I've never really partaken in the business of Hollywood. Otherwise, I would be a different person. I'd probably have seven shows on television. And I just have never done that.

JR: And you were never tempted?

AB: No, I really wasn't. I guess it's because the business and I never embraced each other. If the businessmen and I had a love affair, maybe I would think differently. I mean, you can understand why Steven Spielberg does this, because he's everyone's hero and he's got people coming up to him twenty-four hours a day saying, "What else do you want to do? Just tell us." Nobody's coming up to me and saying, "Hey, come up with any idea you want. We'll build a theme park."

JR: So, how did you avoid getting sucked in by the industry?

AB: I think I got a little bit of immunity because my father was in the business. As a very young child I met lots of famous people and learned not to be impressed by the wrong things. I was inoculated. You see famous people having horrible troubles, and you understand that fame isn't necessarily something to aspire to. If you aspire to get your talent out and then become famous because of it, that's fine. But if you simply aspire to being famous, this town will kill you. It will kill you!

JR: And this notion that there might be an actual muse, alive in Hollywood?

AB: The whole thing about Hollywood is that people are who you think they are.

JR: It's an oddly gullible place.

AB: Yes, because it's built on imaginary ideas and things. It's hard to become the head of Pfizer if you don't have some ability in the chemical world. But believe me, you could become the head of the studio by working in the mail room at William Morris and opening up someone's mail and getting the answers before other people. A lot of people who are big today, that's how they started. It's all built on illusion.

JR: Will any of these studio executives be angry that you're mocking them in *The Muse*? Will they even recognize that you are?

AB: No, I don't think so. All they'll look at is how the movie is doing. If the movie does do well, that will hurt them more than the portrayal.

JR: Is writing comedy hard for you, in the sense that there's no audience there, no response?

AB: I used to come up with all my stand-up stuff alone, and I would make myself laugh all the time. [And] sometimes I would just call my friends [among them, Reiner and Carrie Fisher] and make them laugh, and that would be all I'd ever want to do with it. My agent used to say, "Stop calling people." I didn't have the desire to get millions of people laughing. If I called you up and I got you laughing on the floor, that's all I needed. I've always been that way, almost to a fault.

JR: How do you choose the subject matter of your movies? Do they all have some correlation to what's going on in your real life?

AB: Well, there must be some correlation, or why would I be doing it? *Mother*, for example, was because I had spent some time trying to see my mother as a person who was not just my mother. Of course, what happened to me in twelve years happened to the character in two hours. But you can't make a twelve-year movie. And maybe now that I have a child, there are going to be some things that come into my brain that haven't been there before. Who knows?

JR: Let's talk about this marriage and fatherhood stuff. You were forty-nine when you got married. Was it just that you weren't ready before that?

AB: It's just the lights were green. It was easy, and I always felt that things should be easy in relationships. There are enough natural problems that come along later. I never understood why people would start [a relationship] by going to a therapist. Why would you marry somebody if you're starting out that way? It should be comfortable. It should fit. And this fit.

JR: Was that a problem for you before, that maybe women were too impressed or intimidated?

AB: Well, I don't think it was "impressed" or "intimidated." It was maybe going out for the wrong reasons—because maybe they have seen you in a movie, but they don't really understand what you do. If you're not understood, you know it, and sometimes in your dating life, if the girl's really pretty, you'll put up with that. But you can only put up with it for so long, because you don't want to feel like you're from Mars. Although you don't really mind feeling like you're from Mars, up until you get laid. Then, once you get laid, you don't want to feel like you're from Mars anymore.

JR: How is being a father going for you?

AB: I never thought about having kids before I was married. But it turns out that every good cliché is true. It's the greatest thing. It forces you to live in the moment, which is something that's very good for me.

JR: Because otherwise you'll drift off?

AB: Yes. I could have tendencies to, you know, go to worried places, the "what if" world. Well, a kid won't let you live in that world. There's too much to do.

This little kid looks at you, and . . . it's like that line from Jim Brooks [writer and director of *As Good as It Gets*]: "It makes me want to be a better man."

JR: As exasperated as you sometimes seem in public, you actually sound like you're pretty content. You're not unhappy, are you?

AB: No, I'm not. Once in a while it occurs to me that I might be one of those guys who's sort of had a little more trouble than they wished they'd had, but what are you going to do? Maybe there was something more I could have done. Maybe I should host *Saturday Night Live* more. I don't know. But, by the same token, that would take from me in another way. So, for me, it's like a juggling act. I'm trying to do as much as I can to keep my equilibrium and, you know, still be me. I don't try to remake the world. I just try to live in it.

Good Morning Pakistan:
Albert Brooks on the Move

Terry Gross / 2006

Broadcasted on *Fresh Air*, January 19, 2006. Reprinted with permission of WHYY, Inc. *Fresh Air* with Terry Gross is produced at WHYY in Philadelphia and distributed by NPR.

Terry Gross: How did you first come up with the idea for *Looking for Comedy in the Muslim World*? What was the very beginning of the idea?

Albert Brooks: Well, the beginning of the idea was about, I would say, a year and a half after 9/11. Sitting home, being scared all the time, watching the terror warnings, and being told we're living in a new world. I began to think, "Well, how do I function in this new world? What do I do?" And I wasn't seeing any motion pictures. Nothing was addressing this post-9/11 life we're all leading. It's interesting—if you look at the films that have risen to the top of 2005 they're virtually all set in the past. *Brokeback Mountain, Munich, Good Night, and Good Luck.* . . .

TG: *Capote.*

AB: *Capote.* Every one of them. And I don't know if this is conscious or an accidental coincidence. It seems like people just were not dealing with the world we're living in. And, especially, there's no motion picture comedies that even want to talk about this subject. If a comedy is set in the present it's a teenage sex comedy and deals with, you know . . .

TG: Teenage sex!

AB: . . . getting laid. Right. So it just got to me after a while. And I thought: "How do I even get into this door?" The other thing that was, and still is, when I started writing this—and even filming it—Karen Hughes had not been brought back to Washington. I think her job is now called "Head of PR to the Muslim World." There was nobody doing anything, so part of the premise of course is that the government decides to do something other than, like Fred Thompson says, "All the normal things: spying and fighting." And it was the combination of those two things. Acknowledging that we're now living in a world that is different, and the government tells us is going to be like this forever. And the idea that we're not doing anything to reach people on a human-to-human level. Even if this idea is too absurd, there are ideas that could be tried.

TG: So you go to India and try interviewing people about what makes them laugh. Is that an answerable question? Could you answer it?

AB: Well, I don't know if it's an answerable question. You know, one of the things that I did a long time ago in my career was I started the "Albert Brooks' Famous School for Comedians" to teach people to be funny. I had a test in *Esquire* magazine that you could fill out to see if you were funny. And, of course, it was done as a satire, but I think *Esquire* got three, four hundred serious replies. And the whole point of that is I never believe—and still don't—that I could teach anyone to be funny. Nor do I really believe . . . you know, listen: you can find out a joke that makes people laugh, but sense of humor is . . . I've been trying to make Americans laugh my whole life. I still can't tell you what they really laugh at. I can use my own movies, and see two hundred people falling on the floor and thirty people looking at them. So, I don't know. It's not like tragedy. Tragedy is everywhere. It's the same: you lose a child, you lose a parent. Every human on the planet is going to have the same emotion. Well, maybe not the Menendez Brothers. Most all of us. But sense of humor—not only is it hard to peg, it changes. What people find funny in 2005 they may not find funny in 2006. And that's another thing about humor: it fluctuates. So, it's interesting. In India and Pakistan—well, especially India—the majority of the population is Hindu, and the minority Muslim population is a hundred and fifty million, which makes it the second largest Muslim country in the world. And then there's a tremendous Sikh population. So our crew was made up of all those three sects of people, and as they got to know me, the Hindus would tell me Sikh jokes, and the Sikhs would tell me Muslim jokes. Somebody said, "What makes people laugh?" And my answer was, "The other guy." That's seemingly what people laugh at: the guy over there.

TG: In the movie, in your attempt to find out what makes people laugh, you give a stand-up performance. And part of the act that you do, which I think is incredibly funny, you play the most ridiculous ventriloquist in the world. Your lips are really moving as you're doing the ventriloquism. And there's the standard ventriloquist schtick where the ventriloquist drinks water while the dummy's singing, so that the ventriloquist could show how good he is at ventriloquism. You do this, except you force the dummy to drink the water.

AB: That's right.

TG: It's just absurd. But what I love about this is you actually did this act in your early comedy career.

AB: It was the very first piece of material I ever did, was the world's worst ventriloquist, Danny and Dave. And I wanted to revive it. Of course, you revive it—you know, there's a funny scene later in the movie where John Carroll Lynch, playing one of the government guys, who's like a frustrated comedian, says, "Why would you choose to do a satire of ventriloquism, when you don't even know if they know what a ventriloquist is?" I say to him, "Well, how do I know that they don't know?" He says, "There's no ventriloquism in India!" It always makes me laugh. But Danny and Dave was the first bit that I ever did, and I wanted to bring back Danny to try it out in front of this audience overseas, and of course it didn't go over as well as it used to on *Ed Sullivan*. And then I do other various things. It's my attempt, as I come up with the idea in the movie, to try as varied a bunch of material that I can come up with, so I'll understand what their sense of humor is by what they laugh at. Unfortunately, that premise needs someone to laugh at something. And I have my troubles with that audience.

TG: Now, this Danny and Dave ventriloquism thing that you do—the bit you do in India, in the movie, to see if it makes people laugh—I'll bet when you did it on TV in your early career that a lot of people didn't laugh at it because it's a joke about . . . it's not a ventriloquism act, it's a joke about ventriloquism, and I bet a lot of people didn't get it then, and you might have even bombed, when you were doing it in your real act.

AB: Terry, I have so many pieces of material that people didn't laugh at in the beginning of my career. And, it's going to sound funny to say, but if I used laughter as a judge, I never would've stayed in the comedy field. I just did these things and audiences had no idea who I was. I mean, the first time I ever did Danny and Dave on *Steve Allen*, on the old Westinghouse show, he introduced me as "Danny and Dave," and everyone in that audience thought I was Danny and Dave. But I used to do a mime that came out and never shut up and all he did was talk. People weren't sure of that. This was sort of my early career. And it's interesting, because when I finally got to *The Tonight Show* I'd already done years of the big shows, like *Ed Sullivan*, but when you finally get to *The Tonight Show* then the only person everybody watches is Johnny. 'Cause I used to do bits on *The Tonight Show*, and the audience wasn't sure, but Johnny was laughing, and in essence Johnny was the audience. If the audience was roaring at you, on *The Tonight Show*, and Johnny didn't like you, you'd never be back.

TG: What made you think about taking real bits you did in your stand-up act, early in your comedy career, and giving them to the character that you play in *Looking for Comedy in the Muslim World*?

AB: Well, since the character I play is Albert Brooks, and Albert hasn't been on a stage for years and years and years. I mean, we sort of dress up Danny, to make him look more like he looks like that character I'm playing in the movie. It was this attempt to reach into my old stand-up bag and pull out what I can. Although the bit that I do at the end of that show, that improvisation bit, is a new piece of material. I'm very fond of that. I tried that out, once, on a Saturday night, about nine years ago, when I just wandered in . . . I went into The Improv one night in Los Angeles and got up on stage, just 'cause, I dunno, I've always had something . . . something bothers me about this whole "improv" idea of comedy. I don't know why, it just bothers me. So I always liked the potential idea of a comedian taking suggestions and ignoring them completely. But I never really fleshed it out. The movie is the first fleshed-out version of that routine. Which, if I were performing live today, I'd do every night—it makes me laugh.

TG: How did you train the audience in the theater in India not to laugh at your jokes, even if they thought they were funny? Because for the movie they have to be totally not moved by your comedy.

AB: We trained them with peanuts and a large whip. No. Look, that audience had to be brought in. What looks like takes place in real time is shot over four days. The audience was there for two and a half days, because you're getting seventy angles of that scene. You start out and talk to the audience, and they want to laugh. And they did laugh at Danny a little. And then you tell them, "Okay, now don't laugh because it's part of the movie." Then when you tell an audience not to laugh two people laugh, then everyone laughs at them. So you just sort of have to wear them down. The lucky thing is, it was about 111 [degrees] in there, and by noon, the first day, I didn't have a problem. Nobody was laughing. It even got to the other side, where, you know, "When do we eat?! What time is lunch?!" "Okay, quiet. Don't yell, you can't do that either." The audience in the first two, three hours was there to have fun. Even though in my mind they were there to work in my movie. And we just wore 'em down.

TG: One of the things you're up against in the movie when you're performing is that this auditorium you've been placed in has no bathroom, there's no dressing room, the stage lights don't work. And as I watched this I was thinking, I bet that happened to you all the time at the start of your career.

AB: When I used to open for Neil Diamond, which I did for a number of years, there was nobody to introduce *me*. I could introduce Neil, but nobody could introduce me. So I used to put on this phony voice—"Good evening, ladies and gentlemen"—and try to give myself a host of credits and try to impress them. I always like when they tell an audience "You've seen . . ." What do you mean I've seen? "You've seen him, you've liked him, you've clapped before . . ." You try to do that. In this situation, the Sikh gentleman: "Can you introduce me?" "I'm not qualified to do that. I don't like to talk in front of people." So I'm forced to build myself up with my own voice, which really did happen.

TG: Now, there's a character who you're interviewing for a job in the movie, to be your assistant, and she asks you a question: "Are you Jewish?"

AB: Yes, she says, "You're not a Jew, are you?"

TG: Yeah, yeah, yeah. So is that a fact that you were anxious to let slip, or preferred not to let slip, while you were doing the movie? Did people know you were Jewish, and did that make a difference to anyone?

AB: I have my "I'm Jewish" florescent hat. But I left that in Los Angeles. No. You know, listen: you're making a movie called *Looking for Comedy in the Muslim World.* I am a Jewish filmmaker. I think this is the movie to acknowledge it here and there; it only seems appropriate. It would be like a subject that if I didn't do it, it would be like a cheat. That woman says, "You're not a Jew, are you?" and I think my answer is, "Not at this moment." One of the things, Terry, that I felt I needed to do, more than maybe my other movies, was make as much . . . not hide anything and make fun of myself. And then I thought I'd be okay. If I put myself, holier than thou, in a movie like this, then it would be trouble. Then it might actually look like I'm poking fun at something. But if the central character is me, and I'm the buffoon, and I'm willing to make myself the buffoon; then other people will get into that spirit.

TG: What was it like to actually get permission to film, where you ended up filming in India? Who did you have to go through?

AB: Well, it's a very complicated process. First of all, I had to go to India, initially, for two and a half weeks, to understand it, to meet with one of the ministers. I was taken there by people who have great knowledge of filming there. I started to write this script without going to India, and I just wasn't describing it correctly. It was, like, "The character Albert walks out of his hotel and sees bright lights like Las Vegas," and it's just not India. So I knew I had to go in order to write it correctly. And I had to go, and go through the entire movie, with these two gentlemen, and they had to say "okay." Now, once they say "okay," all that means is you can come in our country. It's not like Los Angeles, or any other American city, that has a film commission, where one "okay" can give you rights to shoot at the dock, or the Empire State Building; it's nothing like that. You get a central "okay," just to come there, just to get visas to the country. You then have to get "okays" from the various cities and states and buildings and monuments. Shooting at the Taj Mahal was like a nightmare of paperwork. But we got it.

TG: What was it like to film at the Taj Mahal?

AB: Well, the Taj Mahal was really unusual, because, first of all, to get permission was, as I said, just . . . I didn't know if it was ever going to happen. For example, they wouldn't allow . . . I mean, in the movie the point of the Taj Mahal is I go there and never see it. The view, where I walk by it, that suited me well for my script. That was as close as you would ever get anyway. They don't let you closer, even if you went there as a tourist, they won't let you near the Taj Mahal with a little flash camera, or any camera. But for some weird reason, they gave us permission. And the other thing is, there is no crowd control. The Taj Mahal is not going to keep people from coming there, just 'cause you're shooting there. So take after take after take after take, and I mean two days of this, were just ruined by seventy people looking in the lens. The movie can handle a few people looking at me—I'm an American; that I can accept. You can actually look at a tourist that you might not normally see at the Taj, and that's okay. But you can't have dozens look in the lens. We were lucky. The second day we were there, there was a huge group of Indian Army reservists visiting, and I think we paid them, some agreement was reached. They formed this daisy chain. This large group of men, that ran ahead of the camera. And just mowed people down. I'm laughing, but people were falling into the grass. Of course, I'm the selfish director! "Good, did anyone look at the lens?" "No, but sir, a man has a concussion." "But did he look at the lens?" It was like the only thing I was asking.

TG: Was anybody in India suspicious of you? Did anybody think you were really like a CIA agent, or that you had . . .

AB: Well, you mean like the mix-up in the story?

TG: Yeah.

AB: I don't know. I don't know what they thought. The thing about India is it's probably the last . . . if there was a Parker Brothers game of countries that still like us, I think India would be the only square left. They like us. The only answer I can come up with is that the British have been such an issue with them, and we're not, so the British take the heat. . . . When they think they have problems, they blame the British. You're not afraid to say, "I'm from America." A lot of the crew went over there with these shirts that say, "I'm Canadian." They didn't know what to expect.

TG: So Sony Pictures, which was initially going to distribute *Looking for Comedy in the Muslim World*, didn't like your title. You ended up moving to another company. What's the story behind them wanting the change?

AB: I think they wanted to shorten it to *Looking for Comedy*.

TG: And get out the words "in the Muslim world."

AB: That's it. Get out the words. I'm sure they would have kept *Looking for Comedy in the World*. I think it was the actual word "Muslim."

TG: Because they were afraid it might be interpreted as offensive to Muslims?

AB: Yes. Here's what they blamed it on. This came about a week and a half after that *Newsweek* story where there was Koran abuse in Cuba. And I think *Newsweek* had retracted that story. That's what they blamed it on. I actually had a conversation with the head of the studio, who said to me, "Look, times have changed, and it warrants a title change," and I said, "Well, times have changed after 9/11—it's why I made the movie." I said, "Abu Ghraib was worse than this *Newsweek* story. Times are changing every day. It's okay to put 'comedy' and 'Muslim' together, I'm telling you it's okay." And he actually said to me, "Look, it's probably okay, but if one mullah in Iran saw the poster and reacted badly you never know what could happen." Now, my reaction was, wait a minute . . . I said, "I've had trouble getting posters put up in Sherman Oaks, you're telling me you're going to put 'em up in Iran?" I said, "This is good news!" I said, "How are they going to see it?" And by the way, when I finally saw the trailers that Sony Pictures made, they had taken out the whole subject anyway. It was like *Bill and Ted Go to India*. It was like: "A comedian decides to put on a show in another country." I said, "Wait a minute, where's my premise?" I think this whole idea of having "Muslim" in the title—and anything to do with Muslim—for a company the size of Sony, that makes televisions, and all the things they do, simply just didn't fly. "Why do we need that?" I really believe that some very high-up executive said one day, who's probably not involved in day-to-day movie business, saw this on a computer printout and said, "We're not going to do this. Why do we need this?" So, they just were worried. I said, "You need to make this movie, because you need to put 'comedy' and 'Muslim' in the same sentence and you'll see that it's a good thing. It's not a bad thing. Comedy is a friendly word." I said, "If the title was *Looking for Religion* or *Looking for Sex*, I could have an argument with you. But where is 'comedy' a bad word? In any language?"

TG: Your film premiered in Dubai at a film festival there. Why did you want that to be the premiere, and what was the reaction like?

AB: Well, first, I'll simply say that it was one of the greatest nights of my life. The reason this happened was initially, the film, which was financed by Steve Bing [who] has a company, Shangri La. In his gut, he said, he was just looking for something, 'cause we found another distributor immediately, but he thought Dubai would be a place to, "look, let's prove to them that there's nothing to be afraid of." And I said, "Well, I never said I wasn't afraid! You prove it, you go! Write me!" But he decided that he wanted this to happen, so we showed the movie to the people who run the festival, and they thought there was nothing that would cause a problem. They showed it to an Egyptian critic, and the critic seemed to just laugh, and I was still very scared to go there. Only because, what do I know? My friends say to me: "What are you, crazy? You're going to bring the movie there?" And it just turned out to be one of the great nights of my life. I'm telling you, in terms of audiences it was like the Cinema 1 in New York. They not only laughed at everything, they seemed overly appreciative of the fact that there's even a comedy out now, especially from America, where the Muslims are not the bad guys; they're so sick and tired of any character that's called a Muslim being a villain. And the other thing (and I learned this by going there) . . . the tension, the post-9/11 tension, is everywhere. It's nothing to do with us. You know, our buildings came down. There's been seven hundred explosions since then, and mostly they've been everywhere else in the world. And 99.8 percent of this planet doesn't want trouble. But one other thing: they also laughed at the languages without even the translations coming up. Of course, everyone speaks Arabic—but there were people who spoke Urdu, and there were people in the audience who spoke Hindi, and it was just interesting, just wild. It was a great night.

TG: So you said that you were actually scared at some point. I don't know how scared you really were, but doing something like this movie has different risks from flop sweat. You're going to countries you've never been in before that you don't speak the language. You're going to countries during an era of terrorism. You're doing something, you certainly don't mean to be offensive at all, but it's possible that somebody would interpret it in the wrong way and find offense. And you're a Jew making a movie about trying to make Muslims laugh, and that might be a kind of sensitive thing too. It's like a new world you're entering in terms of a performer.

AB: By the way, I'm making a list as you're reeling them off.

TG: You're getting worried?

AB: I'm scared reading the list!

TG: Yeah!

AB: No, but that is the answer. All of those reasons. There's no roadmap. Nobody can tell me, "Well, last year the festival showed *Jack Smith Goes to the Muslim World*, and it went fine." They actually told me that in the first year of the festival they showed *Control Room*, the Al Jazeera documentary, and that a sizable amount of people booed and walked out.

TG: Oh, why?

AB: I don't know. But they just . . . that was that audience.

TG: There's a running gag: you're trying to win people over so they'll answer your questions about what makes them laugh, when you first get to India and you're trying to do interviews to find this out. And people don't know who the heck you are, and the only glimmer of recognition you get is when you explain that you were in *Finding Nemo*, and that you were the voice of a fish. Was that what reality was like for you too, that that was the only point of connection, and did a lot of people in India see *Finding Nemo*?

AB: No, because mostly it would be dubbed anyway!

TG: Oh, of course!

AB: Yeah, right.

TG: Oh my God, I didn't even get that one.

AB: That's why, yeah. There's the joke.

TG: That's so great.

AB: See, by the way, that answers your question.

TG: Here's an English-speaking American who loves your humor and it went right past me.

AB: Let me turn to the judge. "Your honor, I rest my case." It's impossible. That's funny.

TG: That's so great. And, if I may say, I was even priding myself on getting a lot of the in-jokes, 'cause I know some of your early works.

AB: But in America, it's . . . obviously, young children weren't watching *Modern Romance*. I have been stopped, more than I think is pleasant, in markets and have cell phones shoved in my face, and "Please say something, please say just anything like Marlin to my son." "Where's your son?" "He's on the phone." That's sorta weird.

TG: Is there a part of you, just even a small part of you, that hopes that your movie, *Looking for Comedy in the Muslim World*, is going to help promote world peace?

AB: Your laughter says it all.

TG: Right.

AB: Listen, I don't believe—I wish I did—I don't believe movies can change the world to that degree. I can't imagine the movie that would bring the Israelis and the Palestinians to the peace table. But, you know, the old Jewish joke: it couldn't hurt.

TG: No, but some people think it could hurt! That's just the thing.

AB: Yeah, but let me tell you something: it is really important to finally elevate these scary subjects to a point where you can make comedies about them. So this is the first one. There should be a hundred. You know, I have young children. . . . If something bad is going to happen to us, it's going to happen anyway. I don't want to see myself and my family hover in a corner waiting for that day. I'd rather get some laughs, waiting. I just think it's necessary.

TG: Well, Albert Brooks, thank you so much for talking with us.

AB: Terry, it's always a pleasure.

Albert Brooks

Scott Tobias / 2006

From the *A.V. Club*, January 18, 2006. Reprinted with permission of *A.V. Club*. Copyright © 2018 by Onion, Inc. www.avclub.com.

Born into show business—his father literally died on stage at a Friars Club roast for Desi Arnaz and Lucille Ball, and his brother is Bob Einstein, aka "Super Dave" Osbourne—Albert Brooks is among the most innovative and respected comedians of his generation. As a stand-up, he made a name for himself on the talk-show circuit, appearing on *The Steve Allen Show, The Dean Martin Show, The Ed Sullivan Show,* and others before settling in for a semiregular stint on *The Tonight Show* with Johnny Carson. After producing two groundbreaking comedy albums (*Comedy Minus One* and *A Star Is Bought*) and several short films for the nascent *Saturday Night Live,* Brooks wrote, directed, and starred in his first feature, 1979's *Real Life,* a prescient black comedy that anticipated the current reality-show craze. Though never a prolific filmmaker, Brooks makes up in quality what he lacks in quantity: His subsequent works include *Modern Romance, Lost in America, Defending Your Life, Mother,* and *The Muse.*

He's also made several prominent appearances as an actor, appearing in *Taxi Driver, Out of Sight, Finding Nemo,* and—in an Oscar-nominated supporting role—James L. Brooks's *Broadcast News.* Brooks's latest effort, *Looking for Comedy in the Muslim World,* was dropped by its original studio, which balked at the title. But its story about an American comic (Brooks) sent on a government mission to India and Pakistan to see what makes Muslims laugh is a lighthearted, self-deprecating treat. Brooks recently spoke to the *A.V. Club* about comedy after 9/11, premiering *Looking for Comedy* at the Dubai International Film Festival, the former and current state of stand-up comedy, and how it's okay to bomb.

Scott Tobias: How did you arrive at the idea for *Looking for Comedy in the Muslim World?*

Albert Brooks: It was a slow process, because after 9/11, just when it came time for me to make another comedy movie, no one was doing anything comedy-wise in movies about this new world we were living in. And I felt that if I couldn't do it, I didn't want to do anything else. I said to somebody, "It's like if a 9.0 earthquake happened in Los Angeles, and then you made a movie about Los Angeles and you didn't include it." So to make a movie about some other subject just didn't feel right to me. I felt like this was the subject that had to be dealt with. Of course, you couldn't do anything [about the post-9/11 world] in a comedy for a year or so after. You didn't even know if there were going to be more attacks. You didn't even know what was gonna happen. And then somewhere around the end of 2002, I started trying to figure out how I could even make a comedy that deals with any of this. How? I started to think about it then, and so it formulated over the next year.

ST: Was it hard to find room for comedy in a situation that inspires such passions from both sides?

AB: Yes, believe me. But you know, there's no roadmap. You can't say, "Well, Jeff did this, I think I'll just tweak that idea." Obviously, I knew I wasn't gonna make fun of the religion or anything. That would be insane even if you wanted to make fun of it, which I didn't, and you have to be very, very careful. First of all, even to shoot in India, you have to get permission from the government, or they wouldn't have even let me in there. I was sort of tiptoeing around the fact that I might wind up causing an issue between [India] and Pakistan—actually, the [government official] laughed at that. He had other issues he didn't want. He told me that they didn't allow *Indiana Jones and the Temple of Doom* to be shot there, and I asked why, and he said because they had a scene where they ate monkey brains. And even though I show that there are cows everywhere, if I had a scene where you stop and the car won't pass a cow, I don't think they'd let you do that. They're tired of that. Certain things like religious beliefs or cultural clichés, they don't want perpetuated. So the issues I was dealing with, they seemed to be all right with.

ST: So the resistance comes from outside the Muslim world?

AB: It's interesting, because the Muslim world is a very large world. There are Arab Muslims, and Pakistan is all a Muslim nation, and even though India is primarily Hindu, the irony is, the minority population places it as the second-largest Muslim population in the world. So when you're in India, you meet many Muslim people, and they have their own relationships with the Sikhs and the Hindus. There's sort of a thing going on there. The Hindus, the guys on the crew, were whispering Sikh jokes: "How come Sikhs don't play poker?" You know, stuff like that. But primarily, because I had to get permission from [the Indian] government, the issues were more about the traditions that they were worried about, that

India was worried about. But I'm the central buffoon in the movie. I'm willing to make fun of myself in all aspects, from being a Jew to being in movies that . . . you know . . . for being in *The In-Laws*, I'll just say that. [*Laughs*] So I think as long as you're willing to do that, really, then things become okay in a strange way.

ST: The film seems similar to *Real Life*, *Lost in America*, and *Mother*, in that they're about these grand experiments that ultimately fail.

AB: Well, interesting that you say that. But *Mother* was more of a success. Because *Mother*, at least you found out who the mother was, and you had some sort of closure to this: "I get it, I know why she's jealous." But you're right. *Real Life*, *Lost in America*, and *Looking for Comedy in the Muslim World* have that same sort of grand experiment gone haywire.

ST: It gives the films a self-deprecating quality that makes them more approachable as well, at least in *Looking for Comedy in the Muslim World*.

AB: Yes, it does. I know in *Lost in America*, there were many people who liked the movie, and many people who said to me, "You know, I sorta wished I could have seen what it would have been like if the characters had bought a cabin and lived there for a year." Well, okay, that's well and good. But my character had to go and eat shit, I'm sorry. *Real Life*, I remember Rex Reed, who I don't even think knew who I was in *Real Life*, of course hated it. It's one of the reviews that I will never forget as long as I live, because it was so insane. He said, "Why would Paramount Pictures give *this man* the money to do such an important experiment?" And I thought, "Wow." It was really one of those things where, "Gee, I guess a lot of people have no idea what I'm doing. This is wild. I'm starting from way behind the pack." On this movie, there were people who said, "Well, what did you find?" Well, you gotta see the movie. It's not finding, it's looking.

ST: How did the film play for a Muslim audience?

AB: Oh, man. Listen, I'm telling you, [premiering the film at the Dubai International Film Festival] was the greatest comedy experience I've ever had, bar none. I was panicked. I didn't know what to expect. I didn't want to go. There was no part of me that was okay about this, but I went, and it was one of those things in life where it's just. . . . Sometimes you're worried about a test for cancer, and you've got cancer. Things don't always turn out so good. But there were two sold-out shows. I went to the opening, and I heard the second show went exactly the same.

Right before the show started, the lights went down, and I'm tapped on the shoulder, and the minister of information, of culture, this sheik, has come in from Abu Dhabi, surprising everyone with his entourage. There are fourteen men in their white robes, and they clear the little balcony out. And he's up there, and they say, "He wants to meet you." So my wife and I go there, but the movie's started, so they just say, "Sit down!" So we watched the whole movie sitting behind him and his group. The laughter's welling up from the first floor, and he's digging it. And I know the Jewish jokes I have coming up. I actually asked somebody, "If a sheik walks out, do they have to walk out with him? Is that part of the custom? Are the average people allowed to stay if a sheik decides he doesn't like it?" "Oh, dear, don't worry, they're not gonna notice the balcony." He didn't walk out. The audience was getting things that Chicago, New York audiences don't even get. So it had a whole different thing going for it.

They're all worried, too. The people on this planet that are trying to live their life, that aren't trying to destroy things, are in the 99.9 percent majority. And the destroyers are destroying everywhere. They're doing it here, they're trying to do it there. People are nervous about it, so they seemed very happy to be laughing at anything, because the few movies that are coming out in general about this subject are all very serious movies, or they're about the terrorist with the heart of gold, or the guy who changes his mind at the last minute. I wish suicide bombers would change their minds at the last minute. I haven't read about that. They seemed really thankful that someone was willing to do it, especially an American. And more than that, they were laughing at stuff. I've got this line in the movie where I'm just talking to my wife about landing at the New Delhi airport. I say, "Nobody was there to pick us up, they stuffed Abbott and Costello and me into a big cab"—*that* got a big laugh. I'm thinking, "Abbott and Costello? Why? How did that happen?" She said, "Honey, everyone's so proud of you, even my mother." "Honey, your mother thinks a Muslim is a fabric." Thirty seconds—you didn't hear any lines after that. Roar. The sheik . . . [*imitates laughter*]. I swear to God, it made me hopeful, just hopeful that a good laugh is going to go down anywhere, providing that you don't go into that territory where they don't want you to, which is the religion, and I didn't. It was never my intention to. I don't know if that would have been okay, if I chose to do that.

ST: Even the few comedies that have gone after subject matter like this have taken a hard satirical angle. But this film has a conciliatory nature. There's something kind of welcoming about it.

AB: Yes. There are a couple of lines in the movie that I really, really, really like, because they're just different. I like when we're crossing the border into Pakistan and I say, "Why doesn't the guy just kill me in this car, I don't want to go with this guy," and the Jon Tenney character says, "I dunno, I think they're comics, not terrorists." It's just a sentence you've never heard before. And the idea of somebody who wants to be a stand-up comedian who normally looks like the guy who wants to kill you . . . I just like fusing those two. It's just funny to me that maybe show business can win out. That maybe the desire to do stand-up can overwhelm someone's desire to blow us up. It makes me laugh.

ST: There's kind of a key moment in the film where you say, "It's okay to bomb." It figures into the plot, but it also sounds like the hard-won philosophy of someone who's been in the comedy business for a long time.

AB: Yes. When I started out, I tried out all my stuff on national television. There were no comedy clubs, but even if there were, I don't think I would have gone to them. I used to do stuff in the bathroom, and then I'd drive down to NBC and do it on *The Golddiggers* with Dean Martin. And some things the audience would laugh at, and some things they wouldn't, and it never was the judge of what I thought was successful. Many of the things that didn't get laughs, I did four years later, when I was known a little bit better, and then they got laughs. And I always felt, in a weird way, that if you only judged comedy on the immediate laughter that you're getting when you're doing it, you're being unfair. Let's say you have trout and you don't like it. Do you never have it again in your whole life, or do you let another chef do it, or do you try it again two years later? It's just not a one-time-only, "this gets one chance and then it must be thrown to the garbage heap." It is an art form, and can change night to night.

And by the way, there are such things as bad audiences. I've heard people say, "There are no bad audiences," but that's just not true. There are people who just shouldn't be together in a room, who produce a really bad audience. Drunks, people who don't want to be there . . . and that's no reason to judge a piece forever. So I think that comedy can and should be done as many times as the comedian wants to do it, and I don't even know that laughter should be the main consideration. It should be how it feels coming out of him, if he feels it's a good bit. I was talking to this interviewer in New York. We were just talking in general about the restrictions of modern-day show business, and I haven't done stand-up in a long time, but I said to him, I felt very lucky that I was not starting as a stand-up now, because even in the comedy clubs, there are guards at the gate going, "I don't think that's funny." And he said, "My God. You don't know! I do stand-up on the side. There's a club in New York, and they're focus-grouping my five minutes." And I just, man, I'm telling you—I don't know how you get a Sam Kinison out of that world. I don't know where Bill Hicks comes from. I don't know how anyone special can go anywhere, because the guards are right in the very embryonic stage. To me, the whole point of comedy is to just go fucking crazy and try things that are as wild as your brain can think of—and do 'em again if they don't work. Do 'em again! Believe me, the audience comes to you.

ST: Is there a place, as a talented stand-up, to do that? Is the art of the comedy album still alive?

AB: I don't know. I just read where somebody got high on the *Billboard* charts with one. I forget who it was. It's not like it used to be, certainly. Comedy albums used to be everything. Anybody who wanted to be a comedian, you listened to them 'til they just fell apart. But I don't think it's what it used to be. I don't know that it's dead. What I'm more afraid of is, there'll always be somebody who gets through, but what you don't want to do is make it so restrictive that people who are starting are just looking for ways to get past the guards, because then they'll automatically censor themselves, and they won't allow their mind to go there. If you want to go out and pee on the stage and you think that's funny, you've got to find a place where you can do that. The only difference is that twenty-five years ago, nobody was on the side of the stage. You could go pee. Right now, someone's going, "What're you going to do? And you're going to take down your zipper, why? You're not going to do that." And that's what I think makes young comedians go, "Look, man, I don't want to have a hassle. I'll just do what I think I can get done." And that's sort of like the chicken and the egg. It starts to change on its own, because people know the obstacle course and are running it.

ST: You're famous for your appearances on talk shows—Carson, Sullivan, etc. Has the game changed there as well?

AB: Yes, the game's definitely changed. I had done a lot of variety shows before I got to Johnny Carson, so I didn't start on *The Tonight Show*. I used to do Ed Sullivan, which had an audience of thirty-five million people. But I got more recognition for doing Johnny Carson, because it was more the people that I lived with. You'd go to the market the next day, everybody would have watched *The Tonight Show*. So it felt more important. But the main difference is that *The Tonight Show* was the only game in town, and the only thing on television where a good appearance would give somebody a stand-up comedy career. And I don't know now that a good appearance at 12:20 on Jay Leno can do that. I don't know the smaller club circuit well enough. Maybe that is what you need. But I'm saying you could make a good living as a stand-up with one home run on *The Tonight Show*. I think there's so much to watch now that getting the focus is hard. There's so much at 11:30 on television that maybe not enough people even know from a Letterman appearance. And Johnny Carson also was a comedy-maker. It was one of the things he did. You know, I love Letterman, I love those guys, but I don't think that's what the Letterman show is known for. It's known for its comedy, not necessarily the comedians that are coming on it.

ST: Do you miss having original material and appearing for no particular reason except to present it?

AB: Well, I'm doing Letterman next week, [Editor's note: "next week" = "last week." It was funny.] and what makes me happy about it is, I've got a bit planned that has nothing to do with the movie. If I do that, it keeps it fresh for me.

ST: Yeah, the problem is that if people are on, it's for some sort of promotional purpose.

AB: It always is. That's why you go on. It's funny. I haven't done Leno often, but I'm always surprised when I'm on there that it's comfortable for me. He's very nice to me, and it feels comfortable. I'm only a couple miles away. I don't know why I don't go around more and just screw around. I'm sure he'd like it, but I just don't. I dunno, I just sort of got out of that mindset.

ST: So do you get a certain amount of latitude when you act in other people's movies? Your character in *Broadcast News*, especially, feels like one of your creations.

AB: To give [director James L.] Brooks credit, I think once he knew I was going to play that part, he sort of wrote it and I played it, but that was his gig. And maybe he liked and could use what I was in a really great way. That's what happens in a movie, if you write for an actor and it all works. You sort of utilize what the actor can really do, even if it's something the actor hasn't done before. In this case, a worried guy who was a downer. But I wasn't ad-libbing on the set. I was acting in a part that he created. But since I came onto the project early, I did have some input into it. Take the sweating scene, for example. [Editor's note: In *Broadcast News*, Brooks's character, Aaron Altman, gets a chance to guest anchor the nightly news, but develops a serious case of flop sweat under the lights.] Initially, when Jim was writing it, he knew that Aaron Altman had to fail, but he didn't know how. And this was 1986, not too long after CNN got off the ground. There was a guy on CNN late at night who was sweating like a fountain. And I called Jim—it was like a quarter to twelve—and I said, "Jim! Jim!" So he turned it on, "Oh my God!" I saw it, I told him, and he put it in. In that case, it was great, because I already had the part and I was able to sort of keep my eye open. So for those reasons, sometimes it can help, but he wrote that, I didn't.

Other times I'm given more latitude, like on *Taxi Driver*, where there was no part written. It was funny, because [screenwriter] Paul Schrader said to me at the wrap party, "That was the only character I really didn't understand." I said, "Jesus, you understood everybody who rapes and murders, and this guy just works in an office. That's the guy you didn't get?" Martin Scorsese didn't ad-lib that on the set. He rehearsed and taped it all in a hotel room, so you played around until you figured something out, and that would go into the script, and that would be what you shot, so you're not making it up on the cameras there.

ST: Are your *Simpsons* appearances all improvised?

AB: That, I make up. They want me to make up as many lines as I can. That's sort of the fun of doing it. I come up with every line I can think of for that.

ST: When you write a movie, do you have certain actors in mind? It feels like the casting is really particular.

AB: The casting's always particular. This movie, I didn't because I didn't know that [supporting actress] Sheetal Sheth existed, and I was hoping someone existed who could do that. I knew I wanted my character to have an assistant who was an Indian woman, and I really looked far and wide. I considered a couple of Bollywood actresses who live in India, but they're impossible to pin down. They do eleven movies a month, and you can't even get one on the phone. So my casting director and I became the current authority in Los Angeles on Indians who live in America, American-born South Asians. I like to write for somebody, but most of the times, the actor or actress I had in mind isn't able to do it. In *Mother*, my first choice was Doris Day, and I couldn't make that happen. Debbie [Reynolds] worked out great. But it actually is easier to write with an actor in mind, because as you're writing, you can start doing the tailoring.

ST: What about Meryl Streep in *Defending Your Life*?

AB: I didn't know she would play that. That was an accident. She was friends with Carrie Fisher at the time, maybe still is, and I was friends with Carrie Fisher at the time, and I had just written this movie. I don't know if I had approached anybody. This was 1990, and I was thinking maybe Farrah Fawcett or something. And so Meryl Streep came up to me at this party and said, "So, what are you working on?" I said, "Oh, I just wrote this movie." And she said, "Is there a part for me?" And I went, "Hey-ha-ha-ha," and then I drove home and I went, "Hey, you know, yeah!"

ST: She's so relaxed in that film.

AB: Is she? I'm proud of that.

ST: Did that require any coaxing on your part—

AB: Yes!

ST: —or was it a surprise?

AB: Once she said she wanted to do it, she just wanted to do it, and it was my job as a director to have her put nothing on. I spent time with her at these parties. I didn't know she even laughed. I only knew her from the movies, and it was one serious thing after another. You know, you see *Sophie's Choice* and *Out of Africa*, and you don't think of a person who's going to sit and chuckle with you. But when I saw this person at a party, I'm going, "That's the person I want in the movie." That was my goal throughout the shoot. "Just be the party person, just relax, just relax." And she did it great.

ST: How much of the way you conceptualized Judgment City was a reflection of life on Earth, and how much was your understanding of what a celestial waystation must be like?

AB: Well, the whole point of making *Defending Your Life* was to take the Heaven out of dying. That's what I wanted to do. Because all these other movies that I'd ever seen always have clouds and Heaven and it's about Heaven, and I didn't want to make it about Heaven. And I think in the most simplistic way, I sort of figured, "Well, if Earth looks like this, maybe everything looks like this.

Maybe we're not just creating this out of pure imagination." Almost like dying is a business, and that's sort of what Judgment City was. And it just became an efficient place, only you had the few deathly perks, like being able to eat all you want.

ST: It's what presumably makes people comfortable.

AB: That's right. It would be to take the shock away as much as possible. Now where you go after that, I didn't bother to explain. That, I wasn't so sure of.

ST: The film is also grappling with how we're supposed to be living. How do you feel it addresses that?

AB: Well, I really do believe, more than anything, that fear is the great issue of all of our lives. I think all of the horrible things are done out of some form of fear mixed in with religion. You know, those two create a lot of issues that people have to deal with. We seem to, as a species, be very afraid, and I just sort of imagined, "What would that be like, if you removed that? How would you function?" I'm not saying you don't keep enough so if a lion's chasing you, you run, but do you need to be afraid going for a job interview? What does that do for you?

ST: Or releasing a movie with the title *Looking for Comedy in the Muslim World.*

AB: You bet. You bet.

I Want a Sense of Reality

Alexander Greenhough / 2018

My interview with Albert Brooks, in March 2018, was conducted by telephone. Seems apt, because the phone call is at the center of his life and work. For pure fun, from what I can tell, in the 1980s he'd call into *The Larry King Show*, a late-night radio show, just to riff. Bill Zehme, writing in 1991, refers to a "telephone circle" of close friends, and describes Brooks watching TV and providing commentary and impersonations over the phone. A fictionalized snippet of this appears early on in James L. Brooks's *Broadcast News*, with Aaron (Albert Brooks) priming Jane (Holly Hunter) with the newsflash that Arnold Schwarzenegger "is on *The Today Show, Good Morning America*, and the *Morning News*—I think he's live on two of them" before going into his impression.

There are plenty of funny phone calls in Brooks's oeuvre—from a 1971 bit on *The Ed Sullivan Show* in which the "smallest, dumpiest, little" Wall Street stockbroker speaks with Howard Hughes to *A Message to Netflix from Albert Brooks* in 2016, where "Albert Brooks" conspires with a kidnapping accomplice. In *Modern Romance*'s long Quaalude sequence, Robert gazing appreciatively at his Rolodex makes and takes a series of calls. His exchange with "Mr. Trashcan"—who asks Robert if he'd mind him asking Mary (Kathryn Harrold) out sometime—always cracks me up. Other choice moments: Jennings Lang as the exasperated, incredulous producer in *Real Life* asking, via speakerphone, "Where the hell is Paul Newman? Where's Redford? Where's Nicholson?"; David discussing "Mercedes leather" with Hans the car salesman in *Lost in America*; Beatrice (Debbie Reynolds) attempting to master a videophone in *Mother*; and, in *Looking for Comedy in the Muslim World*, "Albert Brooks" reacting to State Department liaison Mark (Jon Tenney) using a Bluetooth headset, saying to himself that it's "going to make me die."

That last one is a great example of what I term a "quick cut" in the interview. I asked Brooks about this editing technique as part of an overall focus on how he makes his films. We discussed key aspects of preproduction, production, and postproduction, as well as the origins of the "Albert Brooks" comedy character and the *Saturday Night Live* shorts, which followed his first film, *Albert Brooks'*

Famous School for Comedians, adapted from his 1971 *Esquire* piece—right around the point in his career where the interview begins.

Alexander Greenhough: The Albert Brooks persona emerged as a distinct figure when you began appearing on *The Tonight Show.* How would you describe the character?

Albert Brooks: It appeared earlier than that actually. I didn't do *The Tonight Show* until about five years into my career. I started on network television; I never did clubs. I would try everything out on network television. In 1968, I did *The Steve Allen Show,* then I went to *The Dean Martin Show*—I was a regular on the summer show. And as people didn't know who I was, I sort of played characters. You know, one of the first things I ever did was Danny and Dave, the world's worst ventriloquist. So I had many of those characters before I got to *The Tonight Show.* In 1971, I started to take my name and use that as a character. I wrote a piece for *Esquire* called "Albert Brooks' Famous School for Comedians." And it was done seriously. It was a nine-page insert. It had a talent test. It had fake pictures of a school. The scary thing was we got 2,200 applications. And then I made a short film of that, and that started "Hello, I'm Albert Brooks." That started this comedy character.

AG: That's who I'm thinking of—the character who sits behind a desk.

AB: On Johnny Carson, what I would do is I'd come on as myself, I'd talk as myself, but sometimes I would bring these bits with me that I'd claim were part of the Albert Brooks enterprise. I told him that I was going out of business, and I was selling my material—you know, Albert Brooks enterprises was going under and you could buy a joke, you could buy a prop.

AG: How would you say that comedy character evolved later in the decade, when you began making the *Saturday Night Live* shorts?

AB: It evolved as a way to puncture the bullshit part of show business—"Hello, here I am at my luxurious Malibu rental." An album I did called *A Star Is Bought* was done like a documentary. We got the guy who narrated *The Motown Story.* It was put together with interviews—a lot of stars, myself.

AG: I was going to ask you about the Albert King bit, because that fascinates me.

AB: So there's an example of the Albert Brooks character who's blatantly making an album to get played on every kind of radio station. "I don't care what it takes, I'm going to get FM listeners if it's the last thing I can do." It was an excuse to be that person who wanted success. Whereas I don't think that was me. Although, you know, I wasn't trying to push success away; I just wasn't going after it with abandon.

AG: When you played another version of yourself in *Looking for Comedy in the Muslim World,* why didn't you play the Albert Brooks character?

AB: Well, I did play the Albert Brooks character! The movie starts out where the Albert Brooks character is going through a patch where he can't get work. So it really is him. It's not the character at twenty-five—it's the character thirty years later.

AG: To me the Albert Brooks character from the *Saturday Night Live* shorts and *Real Life* is insensitive, if not menacing, whereas the character in *Looking for Comedy in the Muslim World* is quite different.

AB: I don't see him as that different. He puts on this stupid outfit, like Justin Trudeau did when he went to India. He's confident he can conquer India with these lousy jokes, and he's slowly worn down. Even in *Real Life*, he was worn down, but he wound up burning their house down. In *Looking for Comedy in the Muslim World*, he inadvertently started a nuclear war. He just didn't do it with callousness; he was defeated, but could never admit it.

AG: He made his most recent appearance, as far as I know, in the promotional video for your films when they streamed on Netflix in 2016.

AB: That's exactly right. There I was behind the desk. It felt like *Albert Brooks' Famous School for Comedians*.

AG: I want to talk about the *Saturday Night Live* shorts. How do you see those films as group?

AB: Dick Ebersol and Lorne Michaels came to me in the fall of '74. They said they were going to take over Saturday night. "We're not going to do reruns of Johnny Carson. Would you like to do *The Albert Brooks Show*?" I tried once before, in '71, to get a summer show of my own. It didn't go the way I wanted, so I never wanted to do it again. The one thing they said that was important was: "We're going to do it in New York, and we're going to do it live." As someone born and raised on the West Coast, that never meant anything to me. Why would you stay up until 11:30, because I can't see anything live here, anyway. If someone said "fuck" on *Ed Sullivan*, I'm never going to see it! My idea was to tape it twice, real time. Once at four and once at seven, and put together the best show. Because to me *The Tonight Show* was as live as you needed. If you were bad on *The Tonight Show*, that's what aired four hours later. They never stopped tape. Ebersol and Michaels's plan to make it truly live didn't appeal to me. So I said, "You know what, I'm not going to do that." So, we didn't talk. Then in the early part of '75 they came back and said, "We need you." Because they didn't have anybody. And they thought I was doing the comedy that represented them, and they asked, "What do you want to do? You can do anything you want." I had recently made the adaptation of the *Esquire* article, and I'd enjoyed that, and I said, "Why don't I make short films for you?" The main thing they agreed to, which they didn't like in the long run, was that I could do it in Los Angeles, and they couldn't cut them. Once the show started and the cast found their footing the New York thing became a great part about it. I don't think they wanted a satellite comedian. They didn't like my films being mailed in. Some were too long.

AG: Like *Heart Surgery.*

AB: You know, it wasn't *that* much longer. What could I do? It was a good film. They didn't want to run it, but my friend Rob Reiner ran it. That returned to the *Albert Brooks' Famous School for Comedians* character. And by the way, some of them weren't that—there was *The Impossible Truth* that was done like a documentary short, there was *Super Season*, in which I made up a bunch of shows supposedly coming to NBC, and the only "Albert Brooks" line was at the end, where the announcer said, "Albert Brooks can finally break through from his late night harness and get a chance to make some big money!"

AG: Let's discuss each one. *The Impossible Truth.*

AB: I always liked those old newsreels they showed in the movie theatres. So that's what it was, with the spinning headline. It was just stories that were ridiculous. The voices I got were the real voices. The guy on *The Impossible Truth* was the *National Geographic* guy. The voice of *Super Season* was an announcer named Dick Tufeld, who did all of NBC's season promos.

AG: *Home Movies.*

AB: That was to introduce me. It was meant to come first, but they didn't run it first.

AG: Why?

AB: I don't know. Because *The Impossible Truth* was shorter!

AG: Were they all made before the show began airing?

AB: Two of them were made before they were aired. Two of them were being filmed as they were aired. And two of them were written and filmed after they were on for a few months. I was working into the winter.

AG: It's interesting to learn that it was your intention to begin with *Home Movies.*

AB: I had a first one and a last one. The last one, *The National Audience Research Institute*, aired last. *The Impossible Truth* was supposed to come second, *Super Season* was third, *Heart Surgery* was fourth. And then, quite frankly, as we were having disagreements, I did the one when I was sick in bed as almost a comment on how I was feeling.

AG: For *Super Season*, did you shoot with a crew that shot those sorts of shows?

AB: No. I shot it with a good crew. You know, those medical shows weren't shot that beautifully. You just had to do close-ups. We got the music that was really good, and I got some actors who had sort of recognizable faces. It was designed to feel familiar.

AG: *Heart Surgery.*

AB: It was such a funny idea, to me, to take an ad out and get someone to let you open up their body.

AG: The ending is amazing, where you have this guy who's post-op right next to the airplane.

AB: Those were Monica Johnson's parents. I'll tell you how long ago that was. You could actually get into an airport, sit there, and have a guy wave in a 747. That's the main difference of the world we live in.

AG: *The National Audience Research Institute.*

AB: That was almost the precursor of *Real Life.* You know, that bullshit thing of backing up your comedy with scientific proof. "I'm not just giving you comedy, I am verifying it with Nobel Prize winners." I guess the theme of my Albert Brooks character is trying to reduce comedy to a black-and-white art form where there's an obvious answer. Of course, there's no art form on the planet where there's less obvious answers.

AG: There are direct references to the *Saturday Night Live* shorts in *Real Life,* like the reappearance of Jack from Cincinnati from *Home Movies.* Did you conceive of the film as a farewell to the Albert Brooks character when you made it?

AB: Oh, no. I just did it as a farewell to the shorts.

AG: So after *Real Life* did you continue to perform in the guise of the Albert Brooks character?

AB: No. I would do things as "Albert Brooks" because that's my name, but I wouldn't come on as the Albert Brooks show business character. I would come on as myself. Even in my first record, *Comedy Minus One*—the first part of which was my stage show at the time—I was just doing stand-up. I was talking with the audience, and wasn't really doing that character, who lent himself to individual concepts.

AG: What's the relationship for you between television and cinema?

AB: Well, the difference has basically disappeared. But during my life, it was huge. Cinema was the place where critics lived. Films would be written about. It could get into the culture. People were forced to make an effort; they would have to get a babysitter. Those things divided it from television. Television was free. It was easy. It was accessible. Everybody was on television. But to do a movie took effort on your part and it took effort on the audience's part. It was treated more importantly. Nobody wrote long theses on *Gunsmoke.*

AG: They do now!

AB: Do you think the difference between the two has disappeared?

AG: I'm very attached to the idea of "the movies"—you know, going *to* them. There's that feeling of anticipation when the lights dim and the trailers begin and you don't know what's going to happen. With television, it's something that's in your home.

AB: Cinema is a great experience for all of those reasons. In my lifetime, I watched movies become a worldwide business. A person like myself was at a disadvantage because I was doing a specific kind of comedy and somebody could say in a room, "Well, will they laugh at that in Korea?" Korea used to be Cleveland—"Will they get you in Cleveland?" Some of the better stories, that aren't just special effects, you're seeing on HBO and Netflix. It's harder to see that in the movie theatre. I think it's too bad, but I don't know what to do about it.

AG: I rewatched *Broadcast News* recently, and I was struck by how dissimilar it is from Hollywood cinema of today. In that film, you're watching people think and feel and talk. The heart of it is just three people, with these wonderful supporting characters. It seems so remote from today's cinema.

AB: Listen, there's still independent movies made today. There'll always be independent movies made. But the amount of them diminishes greatly. When Hollywood became a worldwide business you could still have your independent movie that broke through. But it's really hard to get a studio interested in those. They want to put a big bet on the table and they want the big payoff. They're not really in the business anymore of making twenty small things and hopefully four big hits. They're in the business of ten giant things, and five big hits. The world has come into the equation. If you're funding a comedy and your goal is to get worldwide business, you've got to think, "What kind of comedy is that? Why is that going to translate?" You get a person like myself who was very specific, and I was trying to convince people that Americans would go to my movie. I never got to the Asian argument!

AG: Much of your comedy is about America, right?

AB: Is it?

AG: I'm thinking of "Phone Call to Americans" from *A Star Is Bought*.

AB: That's just a blowhard guy. That kind of guy lives everywhere. Take *Modern Romance*: I don't think jealousy is American.

AG: You make that point in *Looking for Comedy in the Muslim World* in the subplot with Albert Brooks's assistant and her boyfriend, whose insecurities resemble those of Robert Cole.

AB: Yeah! They're filmed in America, and I obviously speak English, so they're American in that regard, but if you strip that away I think the subject matter of my films is pretty open. If you look at *Real Life*, it anticipates reality television, and they have that everywhere.

AG: You write your screenplays by acting out the parts and stage directions, and recording it to tape. Before this begins, do you write an outline for the film's story?

AB: I know the beginning, middle, and end. And I know many scenes, but I don't know all of them. Mostly I know my endings. Although I don't always know. For example, in *Real Life* I could tell you it would be a lofty set-up, with a lot of expense, a lot of studio involvement, a lot of scientific involvement. It goes wrong, he burns down their house. I knew that before I started. *Lost in America* I wanted to make because nothing intrigued me more than changing your entire life and having to back out a week later. You know, "eat shit." *Modern Romance* was always break up, get back together, break up, get back together, break up, get back together. This never-ending process that, at times, in people's lives they can't escape.

AG: When you're recording to tape, how vivid is your imagination? What are you visualizing?

AB: The scene. Because I can do the different voices I'll talk differently; I sort of feel like I'm in the moment when it's going well.

AG: Do you discover new characters in that process?

AB: Yes. My most recent writing experience was writing my novel *2030*, which I didn't write on tape. I wrote it on a computer. That was amazing because I knew the beginning, middle, and end, but I didn't know anything. It's similar with tape; I find that the most exciting part of the writing is that if you mold some characters they can take you places. That's the secret of writing. If I'm going to write you, and flesh you out, and I can give you a background, and a current life, and I can understand that life, then if I put you in a Sandals resort in Aruba something interesting can happen.

AG: When you were working with Monica Johnson, was she performing roles on tape as well?

AB: No. We had a very great shorthand. Monica would whenever possible sit with me. She understood my sense of humor, aside from being really funny herself. She was wonderfully creative to do that kind of a thing with, to open up, because she would really, really, really get it, and really appreciate it. Then, she'd be able to throw in something, without disturbing it. When you were on a roll, she could throw out a line. It was hysterical; it wouldn't derail the train of thought.

AG: What was her involvement in production and postproduction?

AB: I didn't involve her. My shooting schedule was always tight. Never enough days that I really wanted. In the writing it's wonderful to stop and think about it; you can rewrite it. Once I had a hundred people there, I didn't want questions like that. I just wanted to go ahead and do it, and sometimes I would ad-lib, but when the clock was running I didn't want to turn to a third person and say, "What do you think?" Like, if you're driving somebody to a place you already know, but the second you say, "How do you want to get there?" the second they give you the first direction you're no longer able to drive. You give up all of your ability. That can happen on a movie set. It's better to do it five times than to do it once and have a big discussion.

AG: Once you begin production on a film, what's the relationship between the script and the film you're making?

AB: I don't ask any of my actors to change the words or think up anything. In a rehearsal period, if something doesn't work for them I can hear it and I can change it. Once it's set, that's what they do. I, on the other hand, will sometimes let the camera roll and do it four different ways. The nest egg speech in *Lost in America* was an outgrowth of that camera just rolling and rolling and rolling. It just kept getting better. I wouldn't do a scene with you and ask you to do that because I believe it always comes out the same. People like to use the word "improv," but mostly improv results in fighting or insults. You don't really get moments of real sensitivity in an improv, because people are fighting to fill a hole. It's always hostile. So I don't ask actors to do that. I will do it in some of my scenes if I think there's still more writing left to do.

AG: What are auditions like for your films?

AB: I bring people in and talk to them. Sometimes read them. When Meryl Streep said she wanted to do *Defending Your Life* there was no audition. For other parts, I meet with people and talk with them. That tells me more than them reading. For example, Rip Torn hadn't worked for a while and he hadn't really done a part like he did as Bob Diamond. It was a different part for him. We just met for a long time. I wanted to know that I could communicate with him. He's obviously a wonderful actor, so I wasn't worried about him reading a line. I was more worried about what the ninth hour of the day would be like. In parts like that I try to understand the person. In *Mother*, before I got to Debbie Reynolds I went through a lot of famous older women, including Nancy Reagan, and read her three times. But I didn't feel it was going to work. Some people you read, some people you just talk to, and some people you know they can do it. When you call Jeff Bridges and say, "Will you play this famous screenwriter in *The Muse*?" when he says "yes" you're done, you don't have to do anything.

AG: You've cast nonprofessional performers in minor roles. Do you cast those on location?

AB: No. Those are important people, and they're all cast before.

AG: What do you think is the job of a director?

AB: Running the cruise ship. One of the jobs of the director—at least, I feel it's important—is to keep the morale up. I try to keep people laughing. I don't make an effort to do it, I just try to make it a very safe place to work. That's one thing the director should do with a crew. I've found that the better I can have a relationship with the crew, the more I get. If you're an asshole and you don't learn anyone's name, that's fine too, but I don't think you get the same kind of work. The best thing people could say to me at the end of a movie was, "Any time you call, I'm here to do another one." Because that meant they liked coming to work. And if they liked coming to work, then I got the best out of them. I think the director sets the mood for everything.

AG: I assume that would be important for you, given the relatively low budgets and the time frames within which you're shooting.

AB: Yes. Remember, in a comedy especially, the crew is your audience. So if you really want to alienate the crew, that's fine, but they'll just walk away. They won't really want to be there if you do that. I like to keep people involved. I like when the sound man says to me, "Oh my God, I thought I'd have to stop the take! You know, the first take, I think it was better for this reason, because I was laughing harder."

AG: How do you approach rehearsal?

AB: Different for different people. Some people need it, some people don't like it. I've done movies where I've rehearsed for two weeks, and I've done movies where I haven't really rehearsed at all. It just depends on the actor. I want to make the actor feel comfortable. So when an actor needs it, we do it.

AG: And when you're acting in other directors' films, do you like to rehearse?

AB: It's the choice of the director. I did this part for Sidney Lumet, in *Critical Care*, and he did something I'd never experienced before. He rehearsed it for three weeks like a play, and then just shot it like that. He didn't like to do more than one take. I was a little uncomfortable with that. Sometimes I'd say, "Can we do it again?" and he'd sort of make fun of me. "Everybody! Albert wants to do it again!"

AG: Do you think that's because he started in television?

AB: Yes, I do. There are many directors who do one or two takes only.

AG: How many takes do you do?

AB: I don't have a set number. I can think of nonactors that I had to do twenty. But it looked great. I can think of actors where I've had to do sixteen. But it looked great. I can think of others where I got it in two. I'm out when my brain tells me, "You're okay."

AG: Technically and dramatically, what do you have to take into account when you're directing yourself?

AB: Everything is prepared. You prepare the shot. You can let someone else walk the steps while you're looking at the camera. But when all of that is done, you have to do what you'd do as actor. I'm not able to watch through a monitor. So I know what it should look like from the rehearsal. And then I get into it, just like you do when you're acting in someone else's movie. Generally, when you think it's really a good take the other actor does too. Normally, people don't go, "That was great!" "Great?! It stunk!" And boy, if the take feels great you pray the cinematographer—and they don't always—says "beautiful." For some cinematographers, nothing's ever beautiful. "How was that?" "Well, you know, it was good but after two minutes someone walked by." "Where?" "Well, it was in the great distance, but you might see it." "But we're in a public place, aren't people supposed to walk by?" I'd say: "Print that, and let me decide."

AG: Do you use video playback?

AB: I've never used video playback. I've only used it a few times on technical shots. There were shots in *Defending Your Life* that had to be manipulated and processed and sent to an effects house. There would be people from the house on set. It wasn't about the performance. So I've never used video playback. It's the economy of the time allowed you. I would rather do it three more times than have everyone stand around and laugh at themselves. To me, it's a waste of time.

AG: Does that mean rushes are important?

AB: Over the course of my filmmaking, I've found rushes to be less important because I didn't have the budget to go back and do something. If I didn't have the performance in one take I'd have it in another one. As I got more of an editing brain I began to understand that better. I had half in one, a third in another, and a third in another. I consider rushes a luxury, but they're only good if you can go back and do it again. I've never been allowed to return to a location once the film was wrapped.

AG: You mentioned your "editing brain." There are many prominent long takes in *Modern Romance, Lost in America*, and *The Muse*. Why?

AB: It creates reality. They're choreographed, like the Quaalude scene from *Modern Romance*, where the camera has to come out of the bedroom and move to the couch. If you can act it like you're doing a play, it feels more real. There's no need to chop it up into all sorts of pieces if you don't have to. The school of filmmaking today, they're not so crazy about that.

AG: It's a pity. There's a long take in *The Muse* which is a great example of elegant depth staging where Andie MacDowell is on the phone in the foreground and the daughter enters in the background.

AB: That's what it is: staged. You hope the actors can do it great and you can leave it like that. Sometimes you run out of time and you didn't get it in the one take you wanted, but you cover it just to save your ass. But it's always beautiful when it's there.

AG: You've said you think of movies as "people looking through a window" and that you don't make the camera the star. Why did you come to this view?

AB: Just to go as far as you can into making people believe it is happening. Obviously, the camera can do amazing things. But if you're sitting in the audience and all of sudden you're aware—"Wow, look at the camerawork!"—I don't think that's a good thing. Everything needs to disappear in service of the story. When I write, I pretend I'm in the other room listening. I pretend I'm outside, looking in, when I'm filming.

AG: So you want a sense of transparency?

AB: I want a sense of reality. I want a sense of believability. For example, if I'm going to write an argument scene with you I can imagine if I were walking down the hall and I heard it. What is it about it that is sounding written, and not real? Sometimes you just take yourself further away and pretend you're viewing it, and you can see. I know fake: like "*no, no, no.*" People don't talk like that!

AG: You mentioned coverage earlier. What's a typical shooting ratio for you?

AB: As I made more movies it got lower because I understood more. In the beginning, I can't give you an exact number, but I would say it was at least thirty to one. I have scenes of *Real Life* that I never put in the movie. There's a funny scene with Mort Lindsey, the composer, who was actually Merv Griffin's conductor. This was an improv scene! I thought of it on the set and did it. It felt too improvy to me, but it was Albert and Mort sitting with pictures of the family, trying to come up with themes for them. It was like, "Oh, no, that's much too nice for him! Look at him!" But Mort, who was so wonderful, did a perfect job. He wasn't made to talk on camera like that, so he could do a minimal, "Okay, well I can make it meaner." That's what I mean about improv—it's unfair for me to ask you to make it up. I don't like to do it. I like to know where I'm going as an actor.

AG: What principles are underlying your approach to cutting?

AB: Performance. I look through all my takes and use the best performance I can find when the camera doesn't drive into a ditch. The goal is to get some sort of emotion across, or comedy across. You're not getting across pictures of buildings.

AG: How do you figure out the timing for those notable "quick cuts" in your films, like that cutaway to the zonked-out guy who offers to drive Mary home in *Modern Romance*, or the cut to the Winnebago pulling out of the trailer park in *Lost in America*?

AB: Sometimes it's the right thing to do when there's no more to say. In *Real Life*, the Albert Brooks character didn't know how to exit and he had to go down. "I think I'll leave frame this way." He couldn't get out!

AG: Speaking of "getting out," you said that you usually know how your films will end. Why do you often include a concluding textual epilogue?

AB: Because it makes me laugh. I don't always do it. By the way, I didn't know how *Defending Your Life* would end for a long time, it was so complicated. At one point I thought my character would come back as a cow and I was working on that. But then this great love story took over and Daniel finally ending up with Julia fit completely into the idea of letting go of fear. Once I had figured it out I realized it never could have been anything else.

Index

About the Editor

Alexander Greenhough teaches in the Program in Writing and Rhetoric at Stanford University.

Printed in the USA
CPSIA information can be obtained
at www.ICGtesting.com
LVHW041809270124
769750LV00003B/37